Arizona

ARIZONA BY ROAD

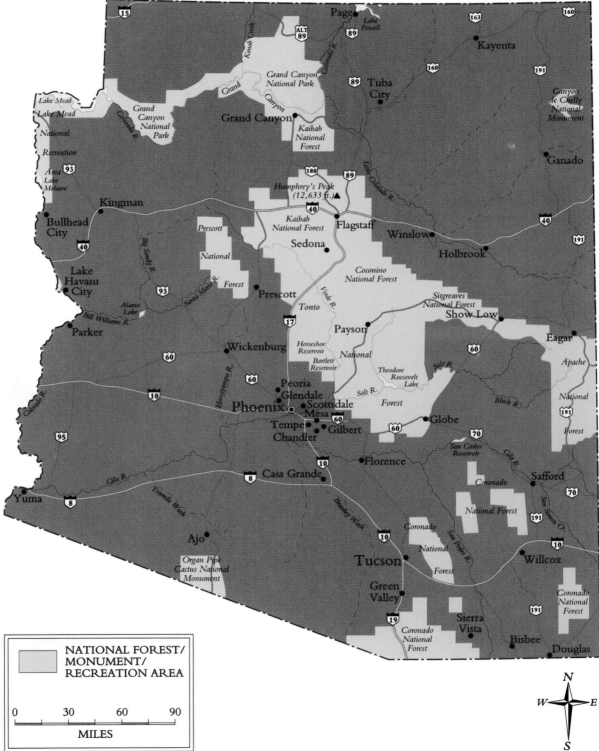

NATIONAL FOREST/
MONUMENT/
RECREATION AREA

0   30   60   90

MILES

N
W   E
S

Celebrate the States

Arizona

Melissa McDaniel and Wendy Mead

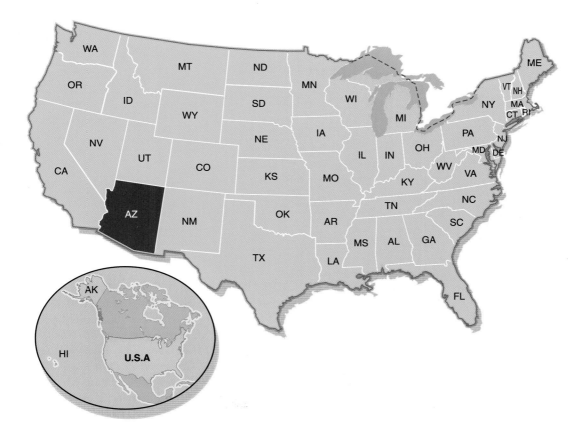

Marshall Cavendish
Benchmark
New York

Marshall Cavendish Benchmark
99 White Plains Road
Tarrytown, NY 10591-5502
www.marshallcavendish.us

All Internet addresses were correct and accurate at the time of printing.
Library of Congress Cataloging-in-Publication Data
McDaniel, Melissa.
Arizona / by Melissa McDaniel and Wendy Mead. — 2nd ed.
p. cm. — (Celebrate the states)
Summary: "Provides comprehensive information on the geography, history, wildlife, governmental
structure, economy, cultural diversity, peoples, religion, and landmarks of
Arizona"—Provided by publisher.
Includes bibliographical references and index.
ISBN 978-0-7614-3398-9
1. Arizona—Juvenile literature. I. Mead, Wendy. II. Title.

F811.3.M38 2009
976.1—dc22
2008006212

Editor: Christine Florie
Publisher: Michelle Bisson
Art Director: Anahid Hamparian
Series Designer: Adam Mietlowski

Photo research by Connie Gardner

Cover photo by Carr Clifton/Minden Pictures

The photographs in this book are used by permission and through the courtesy of: *Getty Images:* John
Giustina, back cover; Tim Flach, 19; Willard Clay, 27; Steve Bly, 57; Rich La Salle, 80, 86; Cliff Leight,
92; Michael Ochs Archives, 129; *Alamy:* Jim West, 74; R1, 98; *Northwind Picture Archives:* 30, 39;
Granger: 35, 36, 40, 43, 44, 47; *AP Photo:* Matt York, 50, 77; Nancy Engebretson, 70; Aaron Mayes,
100; Paul Connors, 123; *Digital Railroad:* Cindy Miller Hopkins, 52; Kerrick James, 109; *The Image
Works:* Jack Kurtz, 61, 63, 82; David Frazier, 66; *Gibson Stock Photography:* 103; *Superstock:* age
footstock, 10, 33, 115; Mauritius, 89; Steve Vidler, 108; *Tom Bean:* 12, *Dembinsky Photo Associates:*
Howard Garrett, 17; Phil Degginger, 105; Willard Clay, 106; *Minden Pictues:* Frans Lanting, 21; Tim
Fitzharris, 26; *Animals, Animals:* 111(T); *Corbis:* David Muench, 8, 96; Marc Muench, 13; Steve Vidler,
16; George H. Huey, 18; Vince Streano, 20; Tom Bean 23, 59, 68; Greg Probst, 32; Bettmann, 38, 41,
73; Corbis, 49; David Katzenstein, 54; Riou/photocuisine, 64; David Kadlubowski, 90; Martyn
Goddard, 94; James Randklev, 97; Theo Allofs, 111 (B), Raymond Gehman, 120; Najlah Feanny, 125;
Phil McCarten, 127; Reuters, 131; Neal Preston, 133; Charles Lenar, 135.

Printed in Malaysia
1 3 5 6 4 2

Contents

Arizona Is . . .

Arizona is hot . . .

The heat is "mind-boggling. When I walk outside I feel like I'm sticking my head in the clothes dryer. It's either hot or it's gorgeous. But we get gorgeous a lot."

—California transplant Mary Jean Flamer

. . . and it is prickly.

"It has been said, and truly, that everything in the desert either stings, stabs, stinks, or sticks. You will find the flora here as venomous, hooked, barbed, thorny, prickly, needled, saw-toothed, hairy, stickered, mean, bitter, sharp, wiry, and fierce as animals."

—naturalist Edward Abbey

Arizona overwhelms the senses . . .

A kaleidoscope of images awaits discovery in . . . Arizona—sycamores shading canyon streams, forested sky islands, giant saguaros, fluttering hummingbirds, rolling ranch lands, tidy vineyards and the wonders of underground caverns."

—writer Nancy Yackel

. . . with its strange beauty.

"Vegetation is not needed to produce beauty in this land for the earth herself is many-hued-streaked with strange bright sands and clays and walled with mountains of rich-hued rock."

—poet and historian Sharlot Hall

Arizona is a young state . . .

"The promising Metropolis of Arizona consisted of three chimneys and a coyote."

—journalist J. Ross Browne, 1864

"If you've been in Phoenix a year, you're an old-timer."

—journalist John Gunther, 1947

. . . that once attracted dreamers who wanted to start life anew.

Arizona was "a blank slate on which they could etch their visions of the future."

—historian Thomas E. Sheridan

Once small, Arizona welcomes new people every day . . .

"Why do people come? In a word, 'lifestyle.' Arizona is a great place to live, work and play."

—historian Marshall Trimble

and faces new challenges because of its rapid growth.

"We need a balance between rural, undeveloped recreational lands and overdeveloped cities and suburbs."

—state land commissioner Mark Winkleman

"I believe Arizona has been, and needs to be, a state of innovation; where we don't do the 'usual' or the ordinary. A state where we recognize our problems and find new ways to fix them."

—Governor Janet Napolitano

Arizona is jagged mountains, gaping canyons, and severe deserts. Its uncompromising landscape made it one of the last states to be settled by white Americans. From the time fortune-seekers first scrambled through its hills in search of gold and silver, it has been a place to reinvent oneself and get a fresh start on life. Arizona holds out that promise still.

Chapter One

Desert and Canyon

Today Arizona is at a crossroads. Covering about 113,634 square miles, it borders Utah to the north, Colorado and New Mexico to the east, Mexico to the south, and California and Nevada to the west. Nicknamed the Grand Canyon State, it has long been known for its breathtaking landforms and landscapes. Equally enchanting are the many different types of plants and animals that call the state's deserts, forests, and mountains home. But Arizona is also one of the fastest-growing states in the nation, with new residents moving there each day. The growing number of Arizonans has led to increased concerns about pollution and the availability of natural resources. In the coming years, Arizonans will have to balance maintaining the state's incredible natural beauty with supporting its explosive growth.

CANYON COUNTRY

The most famous landform in Arizona is the Grand Canyon. This vast chasm cuts across northwestern Arizona. Its eroded pillars, sheer cliffs, and crumbly slopes are dressed in muted colors. Watching the play of

Arizona is quite varied, filled with mountains, forests, and deserts. Here spring poppies cover a hillside in Tonto National Monument.

The mighty Grand Canyon can be up to 18 miles wide and 1 mile deep in places.

light and shadow and the way the oranges and greens and rusts subtly change as the sun crosses the sky are the real pleasures of the canyon. The Grand Canyon is so huge that it is hard to comprehend. "Pick any little section of it," says one visitor, "and think about it. It's actually a cliff a thousand feet high. And below it is another, and another, and another. It boggles the mind."

Size alone can't explain the canyon's allure. Other canyons are deeper and more rugged, but none can equal the Grand Canyon in sheer majesty. After naturalist John Muir visited the canyon in 1896, he said, "No matter how far you have wandered hitherto, or how many famous gorges and valleys you have seen, this one, the Grand Canyon of the Colorado, will seem as novel to you, as unearthly in the color and grandeur and quantity of its architecture, as if you had found it after death, on some other star."

More than 5,000 feet below the canyon's rim, what looks like a tiny stream is actually the mighty Colorado River. The coursing Colorado helped carve the 277 miles of the Grand Canyon to its present depths. But it was rain and snowmelt and streams that assisted the canyon with its width—as much as 18 miles—and carved its spectacular shapes. Geologists also say that the land around the canyon contributed to the size of this natural wonder. Because of the movement of geological faults, the land rose up while the waters of the Colorado wore the canyon down.

This unusual terrain is rich with animal and plant life. More than 355 bird species soar above the Grand Canyon and 89 types of mammals roam its trails. The park's centerpiece, the Colorado River, is home to more than 17 fish species. There are also more than 47 reptile species and 9 amphibian species living within its borders. Some of these amazing creatures are endangered, such as the razorback sucker and southwestern willow flycatcher.

The headwaters of the Colorado River are located in Colorado. Here the river winds its way through the Grand Canyon.

With its many habitats, the Grand Canyon is the perfect place for more than 1,700 types of plants. Western honey mesquites and catclaw acacias can be found along the park's waterways, and pinyon pines often grow in its woodland areas. Only a select few visitors, however, will catch a glimpse of rare plants such as the endangered sentry milk-vetch or the Grand Canyon rose.

MOUNTAINS AND FORESTS

South of the Grand Canyon are the San Francisco Mountains, which include Humphreys Peak, the state's highest point at 12,633 feet. These rugged mountains are a far cry from the typical image of Arizona. There, thick forests of Douglas fir and white fir provide dark, damp homes

The San Francisco Mountains are all that is left of ancient, extinct volcanoes.

for black bears and mountain lions. The region also boasts the world's largest stand of soaring ponderosa pine, a favorite home for tassel-eared squirrels.

Some former animal inhabitants of these lands have been brought back. Threatened with extinction, the Mexican gray wolf was reintroduced to a special area of the Apache-Sitgreaves National Forest and the Gila National Forest in New Mexico in 1998. As part of the plan to save the species, eleven wolves raised in captivity were released into the wild. Their population now numbers about sixty.

The Tonto National Forest is home to nearly twenty endangered or threatened species of plants and animals. Arizona cliffrose shrubs and Arizona agave plants grow there. Chiricahua leopard frogs hop along the forest floor, while lesser long-nosed bats and Mexican spotted owls fly overhead. With its six lakes and nearly 900 miles of trails, the forest is also a popular destination for Arizonans looking to enjoy the great outdoors. There, as in many of the state's forests and parks, a delicate balance must be maintained between welcoming visitors and preserving natural habitats.

Along with its many forests, central Arizona is known for its mountainous areas. The cool peaks of the White, Mazatzal, and other ranges entice hikers, fishers, and anyone else who wants a bit of relief from the heat. Slashing across this region is a peculiar formation called the Mogollon Rim. Here the land suddenly climbs about 2,000 feet. This steep, heavily forested cliff serves as a boundary between northern Arizona and the desert regions to the south.

FOUR DESERTS

In addition to its magnificent forests and chasms, less than one-half of Arizona is desert. But again, Arizona surprises, because it has not just one desert, but four.

LAND AND WATER

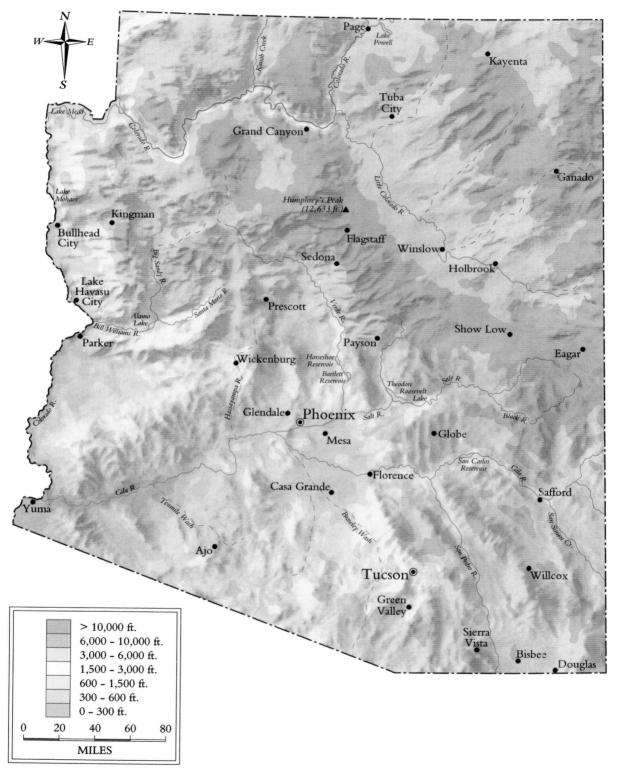

N
W E
S

Page • Lake Powell
Kayenta •
Tuba City •
Lake Mead
Kanab Creek
Colorado R.
Colorado R.
Grand Canyon •
Ganado •
Little Colorado R.
Lake Mohave
Humphrey's Peak (12,633 ft.) ▲
Kingman •
Flagstaff •
Winslow •
Bullhead City •
Sedona •
Holbrook •
Big Sandy R.
Lake Havasu City
Verde R.
Prescott •
Show Low •
Santa Maria R.
Alamo Lake
Payson •
Eagar •
Bill Williams R.
Parker •
Wickenburg •
Horseshoe Reservoir
Bartlett Reservoir
Theodore Roosevelt Lake
Salt R.
Hassayampa R.
Black R.
Colorado R.
Glendale •
Phoenix ◉
Salt R.
Globe •
Mesa •
San Carlos Reservoir
Gila R.
Safford •
Florence •
Gila R.
Casa Grande •
San Simon Cr.
Tenmile Wash
Brawley Wash
San Pedro R.
Yuma •
Ajo •
Tucson ◉
Willcox •
Green Valley •
Sierra Vista •
Bisbee •
Douglas •

0   20   40   60   80

MILES

> 10,000 ft.
6,000 – 10,000 ft.
3,000 – 6,000 ft.
1,500 – 3,000 ft.
600 – 1,500 ft.
300 – 600 ft.
0 – 300 ft.

The Mojave Desert in the northwest is the state's bleakest and driest desert, receiving only 2 to 6 inches of rain a year. Barren, brown hills stretch into the distance. Sometimes, the only plant life visible is creosote, a scrubby evergreen bush that seems able to withstand any weather. Creosotes are remarkably hardy: scientists think some of them are 11,000 years old. This means that somewhere out there is a creosote bush that is the oldest living thing on Earth.

In northeastern Arizona is the Great Basin Desert, a fascinating region of eroded canyons, hills, and buttes. Its most famous stretch is Monument Valley, where strange, isolated rock formations rise from the surrounding flatlands. At one time, the entire area was as tall as the "monuments" are today, but over time the sandstone splintered, crumbled, and washed away. All that is left today are the jagged red spires.

Mostly on lands within the Navajo Reservation, Monument Valley's large rock formations make the area look like something from out of this world.

DESERT GIANTS

Nothing says Arizona like the saguaro. This towering cactus has become the symbol of the state, appearing on license plates and in advertisements. In movies, saguaros even show up among the dramatic buttes of Monument Valley, although they don't actually grow there. To filmmakers, Arizona equals saguaros, so they construct fake ones.

Saguaros grow only in the Sonoran Desert, where they provide homes for many desert creatures. Gila woodpeckers and gilded flickers make holes in the cactus and nest there. Once they have raised their young, these birds move on. Then a cactus wren or an elf owl might move in. The holes make ideal homes because it is often twenty degrees cooler inside a saguaro than outside in the blazing sun.

Saguaros are the giants of the desert, sometimes topping 50 feet. But it takes 125 years for them to grow that tall. Saguaros don't even sprout their first arms until they are about fifty to seventy years old.

The saguaros' arms make them seem human. Especially when the light is low, saguaros can look like forlorn figures in the distance. Perhaps this is why Arizonans have taken them to heart. People still talk about the time a few years ago when a man fired a shotgun at a saguaro believing it to be a human. The cactus toppled onto the gunman, killing him. Many Arizonans felt sorrier for the saguaro.

In Arizona's southeastern corner is the Chihuahuan Desert. This is the high desert, where the sharp spears of yucca plants rise from amid the grasses that take root there.

The jewel of the Arizona deserts is the Sonoran, which spreads across most of the southern third of the state. This is the desert that comes to mind when you think of Arizona, the one of towering saguaro cacti, with their "arms" reaching toward the sky. The Sonoran Desert hosts a greater variety of plants and animals than any other desert in North America. Indeed it is the only one with areas so thick with trees that they can actually be

Saguaros, teddy bear cholla, and other plants grow in the Sonoran Desert.

called forests. The Sonoran is filled with mesquite, paloverde, brittlebush, ocotillo, and cactus galore—prickly pear, barrel, hedgehog, and organ pipe.

The teddy bear cholla gets its name from the spines that cover it and make it appear fuzzy. Far from cuddly, however, it is among the most hazardous cacti to humans. Its spines are shaped like fishhooks, with tiny barbs that jut backward. These barbs hold the spine in place when it sticks into the skin. Sometimes the only way to remove one of these spines is to pull it out with pliers.

Arizona's animals can be as dangerous to humans as its plants. The state is home to several types of rattlesnakes, thirty species of scorpions, and even the Gila monster, one of only two venomous lizards on Earth. Although the Gila monster has gained a reputation as a killer, its bite is rarely deadly, and it will only bite if it's being harassed.

Of course, not all desert animals are poisonous. You'll also find jackrabbits, desert tortoises, bighorn sheep, and mice in the Arizona deserts.

Gila monsters are found in Arizona. They eat small rodents, ants, and the eggs of other animals.

SKY ISLANDS

Even though you are surrounded by desert in southern Arizona, no matter where you go you can still see mountains. These mountains are sometimes called sky islands, because many of the animals living on them are stranded there, just as they would be if they were living on an island. For instance, the Chiricahua fox squirrel, which lives in the cool forests of the Chiricahua Mountains in southeastern Arizona, could never survive a trip across the hot, dry desert to another mountain. If development, pollution, or a forest fire destroyed its habitat, it could not simply move on. It would never survive.

A trip up to the peak of one of these mountains is like traveling from Mexico to Canada, except that instead of having to drive more than 1,000 miles, a visitor would just drive a couple of miles up a snaking road. In the higher elevations of the mountains, around 9,000 feet, the landscape changes from rugged desert to cool forest. Indeed the sky islands are among the most diverse places in the United States. They are home to an amazing range of creatures, from tarantulas to bobcats to coatimundis, including sixty animal species that live nowhere else. More than 250 species of birds find food and shelter in the sky islands. Many Mexican birds, such as the trogan and the painted redstart, never travel any farther into the United States.

The coatimundi, a relative of the raccoon, lives in the mountains of Arizona.

THE JAGUAR RETURNS

"I never thought I'd see a jaguar," says Jack Childs. "I thought it was just something you talked about around the campfire." But in 1996, Childs came across one of these mighty cats in the Baboquivari Mountains in southern Arizona.

The jaguar is the largest feline in the Western Hemisphere. It sometimes grows to 8 feet long. Although these striking creatures once roamed the Southwest, they were thought to have been eliminated from the United States. But a few months before Childs's sighting, rancher Warner Glenn encountered a jaguar along the Arizona–New Mexico border. He photographed it, providing the first evidence in a decade that a jaguar remained in the United States.

The jaguar "is here because he likes what he's found—plenty of game and not very many people, and that's the way we'd like to keep it," says Glenn. The Arizona–New Mexico Jaguar Conservation Team (JAGCT) was formed after these jaguar sightings. As part of its mission to protect and monitor these animals in the area, the JAGCT set up cameras in the Peloncillo Mountains. Using this equip-ment, a male jaguar was photographed in 2001 and again in 2003. The cameras also captured images of a wild jaguar in January and February of 2007.

The JAG Team has also worked on habitat preservation and establishing tougher penalties for killing jaguars. In addition, its members reached out to Mexico to help save these amazing animals, since jaguars living in southern Arizona likely travel back and forth over the Mexican-American border numerous times.

HEAVEN AND HELL

There's no denying it—Arizona is hot. It's not a coincidence that Arizona boasts more places with the word *hell* in their names than any other state. There are fifty-five of them, ranging from Hell Hole Valley to Hellgate Mountain, not to mention several different Hell Canyons.

On average, Phoenix suffers through ninety-two days a year when the temperature breaks 100 degrees Fahrenheit. The first day sometimes hits as early as late March, but more commonly, May brings the triple-digit heat. In the days before air conditioning, this sort of heat was insufferable. During summer people would haul their beds outdoors to sleep. Wily Arizonans put the legs of their beds in buckets of water to keep scorpions from crawling up and into bed with them. Today, Arizonans cope by rarely venturing out into the oppressive heat. They move from air-conditioned houses to air-conditioned cars to air-conditioned offices. Some only go outside for an early-morning round of golf or a refreshing dip in the pool at the day's end.

Many people believe that June is the worst month to be in southern Arizona. It is not only hot, but it is also bone-dry. The ground hardens, plants shrivel, and tempers flare. But then, in July and August, monsoon season hits. On some afternoons, thunderclouds roll in and dump buckets of rain on the parched land. Although the rains last only a few minutes, they bring blessed relief.

But these rains also bring danger, because the parched land cannot soak up that much water at once. Instead the water courses down gullies and dry creek beds, sometimes creating dangerous flash floods. In August 2005 heavy rains dropped as much as 4 inches of water on some parts of southern Arizona. The Tucson area was especially hard hit, forcing the evacuation of forty-six people. Two of them had to be rescued by a helicopter after they were trapped on the porch of a home by the floodwaters.

A great way to escape the Arizona heat is to cool off in the water at Oak Creek in Slide Rock State Park.

HELL IN ARIZONA

It was part of the frontier spirit never to take oneself too seriously. So when the Arizona Booster said, "Arizona needs only water and climate to make it a paradise," the skeptical listener responded, "Yes, that's all hell needs, too."

The de-vil was giv-en per-mis-sion one

day To se-lect him a land for his own spe-cial

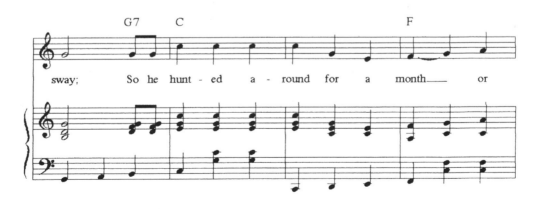

sway; So he hunt-ed a-round for a month___ or

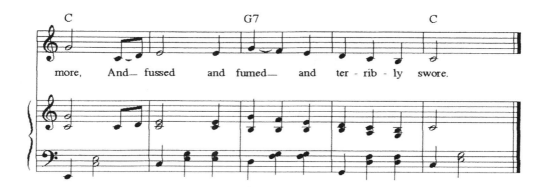

more, And— fussed and fumed— and ter - rib - ly swore.

He at last was delighted a country to view
Where the prickly pear and the mesquite grew.
With a survey brief, without further excuse,
He stood on the bank of the Santa Cruz.

He studded the land with the prickly pear,
And scattered the cactus everywhere;
The Spanish dagger, sharp-pointed and tall,
And at last the chollas to outstick them all.

He filled the river with sand 'til 'twas almost dry,
And poisoned the land with alkali;
And promised himself on its slimy brink
To control all who from it should drink.

He saw there was one improvement to make,
So he imported the scorpion, tarantula, and snake,
That all that might come to this country to dwell,
Would be sure to think it was almost hell.

He fixed the heat at a hundred and 'leven,
And banished forever the moisture from heaven;
And remarked as he heard his furnaces roar
That the heat might reach five hundred more.

Winter sees milder rains and milder temperatures. In December and January in southern Arizona, temperatures average in the sixties, with lows rarely dipping below freezing. For decades Arizona's pleasant winters have been enticing visitors. Those who come get more than comfortable weather. Each evening, as the blinding light of day begins to fade, the sky puts on a dazzling show. It explodes in pinks and peaches and purples, which change quickly, so that each minute prompts more "oohs" and "aahs." Arizona sunsets are neon and brilliantly colored. They act like magnets, drawing people out of their homes and luring motorists off the road to watch. No matter what you're doing, an Arizona sunset is always worth stopping for.

The sun sets over the Grand Canyon, transforming the sky to vivid pink and purple.

With the warm, dry spring come spectacular wildflower displays. Practically overnight the muted browns and olive greens of the desert are overwhelmed with expanses of blue lupine or brilliant yellow desert marigold. "It's like a volcano of gold," exclaimed one man upon seeing the fields of Mexican gold poppies in Picacho Peak State Park.

After the wildflowers of March have faded, May and June bring dazzling cactus blossoms. The bright scarlet blooms that emerge from a tangle of spines on the claret cup cactus are almost as big as the plant itself. And at the end of the season, delicate white flowers bloom atop the giant saguaros, only to wilt after one day.

Mexican gold poppies explode with color in springtime in Arizona.

Farther north in Arizona, the climate is much milder. Towns such as Sedona and Prescott enjoy four distinct seasons, each of them pleasant. From the aspens blazing yellow against a brilliant blue autumn sky to the beautiful dustings of snow in the winter, Arizona can seem like heaven. A man who fled the frigid winters and humid summers of Chicago for Sedona explained his decision: "One word: weather."

DUST AND HAZE

It used to be that people moved to Arizona to enjoy the clean desert air—and many still do flock to the state's more rural areas. But its cities in the south are another story. All too often a pillow of brown haze nestles against southern Arizona's jagged mountains. Much of this pollution comes from car and truck exhaust. And when tiny particles of dust and exhaust settle onto the road in Arizona's dry climate, they get kicked back up into the air by passing cars.

More and more city-dwelling Arizonans are suffering from breathing problems, headaches, and stinging eyes, and many blame the particle pollution. Although Arizonans are using cleaner fuel, this won't solve the problem. People would have to drive less to reduce the amount of dust particles churned into the air, and that seems unlikely. Phoenix area residents drove 85 million miles a day in 2005, about a 70 percent increase from the 50 million miles driven a decade earlier.

The Phoenix area also has a number of days each year when it has high levels of ozone pollution. This type of pollution is created by a combination of vehicle exhaust and other chemicals interacting with heat and sunlight to form ozone. Much higher above the earth, a layer of ozone gas protects the earth. On the ground, however, it can cause health problems. On high-ozone alert days, children and others with breathing problems such as asthma are advised to stay indoors. "With bad air we need to be a little more cautious on how often we're out," says Charles "Chip" Finch, a Phoenix area emergency-room physician.

To improve the city's air, Phoenix has several initiatives under way. It has started expanding its mass transit system by putting in a light-rail line and adding new bus lines. To encourage its workers to travel by bus, the city covers their fares and offers them alternative work schedules to lessen rush-hour traffic congestion and pollution.

Besides Phoenix's Maricopa County, other areas in the state are also having air pollution problems because of their extensive growth. Pima and Pinal counties have also been working to keep their air clean. Throughout the state, the government is looking for ways to improve air quality and ease traffic congestion. In 2007 the Arizona legislature passed a bill that addressed both particle and ozone pollution. Among many other initiatives, it called for a cleaner-burning gasoline to be sold during the summer months in some areas, and to have the sides of certain roadways paved to cut down on dust. "Clean air is not just a matter of making the sky more blue," says Governor Janet Napolitano. "Our air quality has a big effect on the health and well-being of Arizonans."

Chapter Two

Becoming Arizona

Arizona is a young state—it was the last of the lower forty-eight states to enter the Union. But humans have lived in the region for thousands of years, giving Arizona a rich and fascinating history. The stories of some of the earliest cultures, such as the Ancestral Pueblo people (once known as the Anasazi) have been pieced together by what they left behind and the tales passed down by generations of other native peoples.

THE FIRST ARIZONANS

The first people to arrive in what is now Arizona were hunters who wandered into the area 12,000 years ago. They stalked the camels, bison, antelope, and other large animals that thrived on what was then the region's grassy plains.

As the climate grew drier, deserts replaced the grasslands. The large animals died off, and people turned to gathering nuts and berries and hunting smaller animals, such as deer and rabbits. More than three thousand years ago, they learned how to farm. Growing corn, beans, and squash enabled them to settle into permanent villages.

One of the earliest groups to settle Arizona was the Ancestral Pueblo people. Their dwellings looked much like those illustrated here.

Over time, they developed into several distinct cultures, including the Hohokam, the Ancestral Pueblo people, the Mogollon, and the Sinagua. Each of these groups created a complex civilization. They sometimes built pueblos—stone buildings, some as high as five stories high—and made artful pottery with dazzling decorations. They grew crops and traded goods with one another and with Indians in Mexico. The Hohokam even dug a vast system of irrigation canals from the Salt River, enabling them to farm in the Sonoran Desert. They also left their mark on the area by creating numerous carvings on rocks, known as petroglyphs. These artworks can still be seen at the Painted Rocks Petroglyph Site near Gila Bend. Archaeologists also discovered ball courts at some Hohokam sites, which suggested a possible link to the native peoples of Central America. There was no evidence, however, that these courts were used to play games.

The Mogollon lived in the southeastern part of Arizona and in what is now New Mexico. At first they lived in simple pit houses or caves; later, they built structures, known as cliff dwellings, into the sides of cliffs. The Ancestral Pueblo people created similar structures in the later years of their culture. Along with these buildings, archaeologists discovered round chambers called kivas, which are believed to have been used for ceremonies.

Pictographs from an early group of people in Arizona decorate a cliff side.

On the Navajo reservation today, it is still possible to see remains of Ancestral Pueblo people's cliff dwellings. One of the most famous is called the White House ruin in Canyon de Chelly. The group's previous name, the Anasazi, actually comes from the Navajo language, which has been translated to mean "ancient enemies" or "ancient ones."

In central Arizona the Sinagua flourished in the Verde Valley and near the San Francisco Mountains. Their name came from the Spanish words for "without water," and they are thought to have interacted with several other ancient peoples,

Ancestral Pueblo people created a settlement known today as the White House ruin in Canyon de Chelly.

including the Ancestral Pueblo people and the Mogollon. Like the Ancestral Pueblo people and the Mogollon, the Sinagua developed an advanced style of architecture. They built what is now referred to as Montezuma Castle, a five-level cliff dwelling made of limestone, wood, and plaster. Located south of Flagstaff, the area is now a national monument.

One by one, between 1200 and 1450 CE, these cultures disappeared. No one is quite sure why. In some cases drought may have been the culprit; in other cases, perhaps it was disease or warfare. In many places it looks as though the American Indians simply walked away from their homes, leaving everything behind. Of course, all of these people did not simply vanish. The Ancestral Pueblo people are believed to be the ancestors of the Hopi, who live on the high mesas of northeastern Arizona. The Hohokam probably became the modern desert peoples known as the Pima and the Tohono O'odham.

The Navajo and Apache began arriving in the Southwest, possibly as early as 1100 CE, from present-day Canada and Alaska. The Navajo settled among the buttes and canyons of northeastern Arizona, where they grew crops and raised sheep. The Apache headed to the mountains farther south. There the men hunted game, and the women gathered nuts and berries.

THE SPANIARDS ARRIVE

By the 1500s Spain had gained control of Mexico. The Spaniards often heard tales of fantastic golden cities to the north. In 1539 an expedition led by Fray (father) Marcos de Niza set out in search of these fabled cities, called the Seven Cities of Cíbola. Spanish explorer, Francisco Coronado, also looked for these cities. One of his men, García López de Cárdenas, left Coronado to investigate rumors of a great river. When Cárdenas gazed into the Grand Canyon, however, the "great river" at the bottom appeared to be little more than a stream. The Spaniards were looking for riches. To them the Grand Canyon was nothing but an impassable barrier, so Cárdenas turned around to catch up with the others. Coronado went all the way to present-day Kansas before finally realizing that the legendary cities were, in fact, only a legend.

In the following decades, only a handful of Spanish expeditions passed through Arizona. For Europeans the region seemed to offer little but unbearable heat. The few who stayed were missionaries seeking to convert the American Indians to Christianity. In 1629 missionaries arrived at the Hopi mesas. They forced the American Indians to build mission churches, work the land, and learn Spanish culture. They even forbid the American

Indians to practice their own religion. When the Pueblo peoples in New Mexico rose up against the Spaniards in 1680 and drove them out, the Hopi also rebelled. Although the Spaniards later regained control of northern New Mexico, the missionaries never returned to the Hopi villages.

Missionaries had better luck in southern Arizona, largely because of the efforts of a priest named Eusebio Francisco Kino. Father Kino was humble and compassionate. He treated the Pima and Tohono O'odham peoples with kindness and respect. He taught them new farming techniques and showed them how to raise cattle and sheep. Kino eventually established at least twenty-four missions in northern Mexico and southern Arizona, including San Xavier del Bac, near present-day Tucson.

The goodwill that Kino established did not survive his death. Some of the missionaries who replaced him treated the American Indians cruelly. In 1751 the American Indians fought back, killing more than one hundred priests, ranchers, and other settlers. To prevent future uprisings, the Spaniards built a fort at Tubac. This was Arizona's first white settlement.

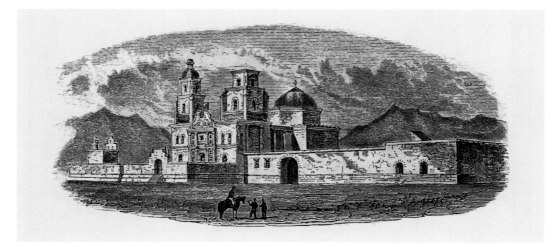

Father Eusebio Francisco Kino founded the San Xavier del Bac Mission around 1700.

CHANGING FLAGS

In 1810 Mexico began a long and bloody struggle for independence from Spain. When Mexico finally triumphed in 1821, Arizona was suddenly part of a new country. This made little difference to most people in this remote region. They simply lowered the Spanish flag and raised the Mexican one.

In 1848 most of Arizona changed flags again. The United States had just won a war with Mexico. As part of the Treaty of Guadalupe Hidalgo that concluded the war, Mexico ceded to the United States a huge swath of land from Texas to California. Arizona was part of the bargain. It eventually became part of the Territory of New Mexico. To Americans, Arizona was an unknown wilderness, nothing but dreaded country one had to cross to reach California. The army sent out parties to scout and map the region in 1851.

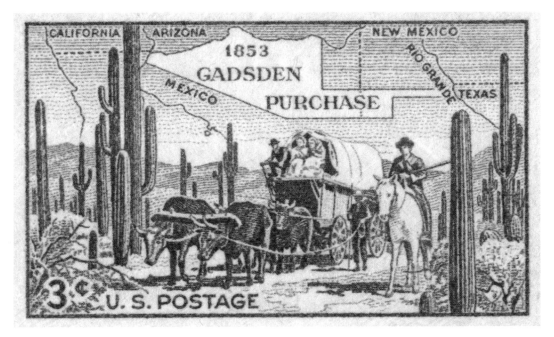

A 1953 postage stamp commemorates the 1853 Gadsen Purchase.

Two years later the United States bought the southernmost part of Arizona from Mexico in the Gadsden Purchase, which was signed in 1853 and ratified the following year.

For nearly a decade Arizona remained part of the Territory of New Mexico. The first effort to make Arizona a separate territory came in 1856, when a group of western New Mexico Territory residents asked Congress to create the Territory of Arizona, but they were unsuccessful. In 1862 a special bill to make the area a U.S. territory, called the Arizona Organic Act, passed in the U.S. House of Representatives and the Senate. President Abraham Lincoln signed the act the next year, during one of the most difficult times in American history—the Civil War.

THE CIVIL WAR

Although few may associate Arizona with the Civil War, the state was involved in the conflict. At the beginning of the war, Arizona was still a part of the Territory of New Mexico, which was of interest to both sides. The Confederate Army wanted to occupy the region to ensure that they would have a route to California's gold fields, while the Union Army wanted to prevent that from happening. In February 1862 Confederate soldiers took control of Tucson. Two months later Union and Confederate soldiers faced off in one of the westernmost battles of the war. The fighting—called the Battle of Picacho Pass—occurred near Picacho Peak, north of Tucson, on April 15, 1862. A group of Union soldiers on a scouting mission for their cavalry unit encountered Confederate scouts. The skirmish lasted about ninety minutes and left three Union soldiers dead.

Union forces also clashed with American Indians in the region. In July 1862 about one hundred volunteers from California who were on their way to the San Simeon River reached the Apache Pass in the

Chiricahua Mountains. There they encountered resistance, not from the Confederate troops they were expecting, but from the Chiricahua Apache.

The soldiers were attacked by a group of Apache led by Cochise and Mangas Coloradas on July 15, 1862. Using small cannons known as howitzers, they were eventually able to drive off the Apache. To protect troops and supply lines in the area, the Union Army decided to build a fort near the scene of this battle. Even after the war, Fort Bowie was a command center for the military's battles with American Indians in the region.

The Union Army also brought many African Americans to the state. Known as Buffalo Soldiers, these men had fought in segregated units during the Civil War, and after the war ended, some of their regiments

Buffalo Soldiers stand at ease at Fort Lincoln, Arizona, in 1865.

were sent west. They served at many sites in Arizona, including Fort Huachuca near Sierra Vista, which remains an active U.S. Army base today. In addition to helping secure the Wild West, the Buffalo Soldiers also provided military support in the army's campaigns against the Apache.

Not long after the Civil War ended, a former soldier came to the state for a completely different mission. In 1869 Major John Wesley Powell, who had lost his right arm during the Civil War, led the first expedition down the Colorado River, all the way through the Grand Canyon. For three months the expedition boats were buffeted by rapids and battered against rocks. Powell's spellbinding reports introduced the rest of the country to the splendors of the canyon. It wasn't long before tourists started trickling in.

Major John Wesley Powell and his team navigate the Colorado River on their 1869 expedition through the Grand Canyon.

THE INDIAN WARS

As whites began arriving in Arizona, the army set out to subdue the American Indians who sometimes raided white settlements. These raids were conducted in part to obtain weapons, livestock, and other goods. Revenge for attacks against their people was also a motivation behind some American Indians' clashes with whites.

In 1863 Colonel Kit Carson was ordered to round up the Navajo in the area. He took the job seriously, chasing the Navajo through the canyons where they lived, burning their crops, and destroying their livestock. Facing starvation, the Navajo had no choice but to surrender. Carson then forced them to take a 300-mile trek during the dead of winter in 1864 to a desolate spot in eastern New Mexico called Bosque Redondo. Without adequate food or clothing, hundreds died on what the Navajo call the Long Walk.

In 1868 after thousands more Navajo had died during a smallpox epidemic or starved to death at Bosque

American frontiersman Kit Carson followed orders to initiate the Navajo Long Walk to New Mexico in 1864.

Redondo, they were given a reservation in their homeland. When they arrived once more in Arizona, "we felt like talking to the ground, we loved it so," said Navajo leader Manuelito.

Meanwhile, in southern Arizona, a bloody conflict was raging between the U.S. Army and a band of Chiricahua Apache led by Cochise. During ten years of skirmishes, Cochise never lost a battle. He surrendered in September 1871, however, because of the toll that the struggle was taking on his band's women and children. But the following spring Cochise escaped when he learned that his people were to be transferred to a reservation in New Mexico. He surrendered for a second time that summer, when a reservation was created for his people in Arizona.

Giving themselves up to the white authorities did not always guarantee the safety of American Indians. For example, more than one hundred Pinal and Aravaipa Apache, mostly women and children, were killed near Tucson in what is now called the Camp Grant Massacre. They had settled at the camp, a U.S. Army facility, in the winter of 1871. Tensions arose between the Pinal and Aravaipa Apache and the area residents because the residents believed that the Apache were responsible for some of the raids in the area. In April a large group of men, including some of Tucson's famous pioneers, Mexican Americans, and about ninety members of the Tohono O'odham, traveled to the camp and launched their own raid on the Apache. Apache leader Eskiminzin and his young daughter were among the only survivors.

Despite the violent fate of the Pinal and Aravaipa Apaches at Camp Grant, other Arizona tribes continued to surrender one by one. Finally only a small band of Apache led by Geronimo remained free. Geronimo's wife and three children had been killed by bounty hunters in 1858. "I could not call back my loved ones," he later declared, "but I could rejoice in this revenge." Geronimo hardened into a great warrior. His pride and determination became legendary. In 1886 thousands of U.S. troops were after him and his band. Geronimo avoided capture for months before finally surrendering in September. He was sent to a prison camp in Florida and later went to live on a reservation in Oklahoma.

Geronimo was a great American-Indian warrior who fought to protect his people's native land.

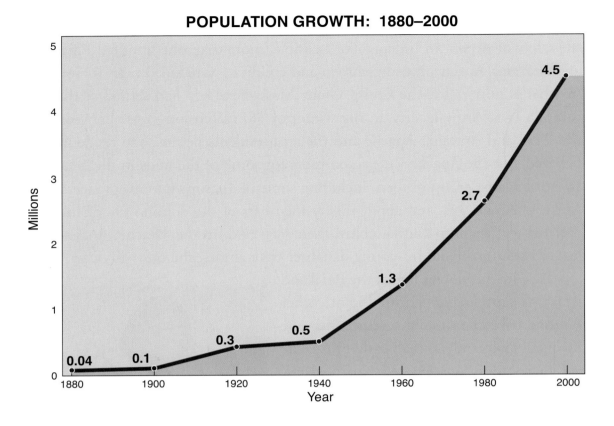

POPULATION GROWTH: 1880–2000

THE BIRTH OF PHOENIX

In the mid-1800s a prospector named John W. "Jack" Swilling was riding through the Salt River Valley when he noticed the remnants of the canals that the Hohokam had dug one thousand years earlier. Swilling realized that if farms had once covered the desert floor, they could again. He had the ditches rebuilt and irrigated the land, and soon wheat and barley were poking up from the once-arid soil. The town that grew up around the rebuilt canals was named Phoenix, after the mythical bird that dies in a burst of flames and then rises again from its ashes.

This illustration of Phoenix was drawn by C. J. Dyer in 1885, four years after the city was incorporated.

Cattle ranching was also on the rise in Arizona. Between 1870 and 1890 the number of cattle grazing on Arizona's meadows and grass-lands leaped from 5,000 to 1.5 million. After the railroads were built in the late 1800s, Arizona farmers and ranchers were better able to ship their goods to market.

THE WILD WEST

Although some families moved to Arizona to farm and put down roots, many more young men drifted into the territory in search of adventure and a new start in life. They were seeking their fortunes, and they were seeking freedom. In many cases *freedom* meant freedom from the law.

Pioneer Arizona was rough and lawless. In 1862 army captain John C. Cremony reported that in Tucson, "Men walked the streets with double-barreled shotguns, hunting each other as sportsmen hunt for game. In the graveyard there were 47 graves of white men in 1860, and of that number only 2 had died natural deaths."

Few places were wilder than the mining boomtowns. Gold was discovered along the Gila River in 1858. Almost overnight a thousand fortune hunters rushed into the area. In less than two years the gold was tapped out, and the disappointed prospectors moved on to their next dream.

This pattern was repeated again and again. In 1877 Ed Schieffelin struck silver. Soon, the town of Tombstone sprang up. Its streets were filled with gamblers and gunfighters, drunkards and thieves. In Tombstone's violent early days, it was often hard to tell the good guys from the bad guys. City marshal Virgil Earp and his brothers, Wyatt and Morgan, both deputy sheriffs, got into Tombstone's most famous shoot-out one afternoon in 1881.

Arizona's early years attracted wild and rough frontiersmen seeking fortune in Arizona's mines.

THE LOST DUTCHMAN MINE

Arizona's mining days are the stuff of legend. Stories abound about fortunes made—and lost—overnight. One tall tale still looms large in the minds of Arizonans.

People say that in the 1870s, Jacob Waltz, whom locals called the Dutchman, made a fabulous gold strike in the rugged Superstition Mountains east of Phoenix. Whenever he came to town, he paid for his purchases with gold. Waltz sometimes bragged about the strike, but swore up and down that he would never tell anyone where it was. Folks asked, begged, and threatened, but he never breathed a word. Some say that Waltz killed anyone who followed him into the mountains.

Although Waltz is long gone, the legend lives on. To this day, fortune hunters scramble up the Superstition's peaks and into its ravines, searching for the Dutchman's lost mine.

Less optimistic souls just think it's a great story. Every March you'll find some of them in Apache Junction for the Lost Dutchman Gold Mine Superstition Mountain Trek. During the daylong festivities, some folks head out on a grueling hike through the mountains. Others prefer to stick behind and eat fresh-baked bread, pan for gold, and enjoy a rousing pageant about the legend of the Lost Dutchman. The night concludes with brilliant fireworks over the dark, craggy hills.

The Earp brothers, along with Doc Holliday, faced off against two members of the Clanton gang and brothers Frank and Tom McLaury, all of whom were allies of Cochise County sheriff Johnny Behan. After the thirty-second showdown, three men lay dying and three were wounded, and the gunfight at the O.K. Corral was on its way to becoming an American legend.

DOWN IN THE MINES

Unlike the silver and gold strikes, copper mining had a lasting impact on Arizona and became one of its chief industries. Many people got rich from copper, but not the men who toiled hundreds of feet underground to mine it. There, amid dim light and hot, foul air, they blasted the ore out of the earth. It was dangerous work. Explosions, cave-ins, and fires took many lives.

Eventually some miners joined unions to try to force the mine owners to improve working conditions. In 1917 miners in Bisbee, the state's leading copper town, went on strike. In response, a group of armed men rounded up the strikers. The more than one thousand strikers who refused to return to work were forced into railroad cars and shipped off to New Mexico, in what is known as the Bisbee Deportation. Few ever returned, and afterward the unions never gained much power in Arizona.

INTO THE TWENTIETH CENTURY

By 1910 Arizona was home to more than 200,000 people. Arizonans had long been clamoring for statehood. On Valentine's Day, 1912, they finally got their wish, becoming the forty-eighth state in the Union.

Many Arizonans had also been seeking a more dependable supply of water to irrigate their fields. In 1911 the Theodore Roosevelt Dam was completed on the Salt River, and the valley blossomed. In the coming decades, dams would slow rivers across the state, providing Arizonans with water, flood control, and cheap electric power.

Early in the twentieth century, Arizona's fortunes were linked to those of the copper industry. During World War I, demand for copper was high, so prices were high and Arizona prospered. During the Great Depression of the 1930s, however, copper prices tumbled, and Arizona suffered along with the rest of the nation.

Then, in 1941, the Japanese attacked Pearl Harbor in Hawaii, and the United States entered World War II. Suddenly Arizona was back in business, as the military demanded huge quantities of the state's three most important products—copper, cattle, and cotton. The military also built air bases in Arizona to take advantage of the clear skies.

In 1912 Arizonans celebrated statehood with a parade in downtown Phoenix.

Not everyone prospered from the war. For some Americans, war brought hardship. All along the West Coast, people of Japanese descent were forced from their homes and into camps, out of fear that they might be loyal to Japan instead of the United States. So many Japanese Americans were herded into a camp in Poston, Arizona, that for a time, it was the state's third-largest city. Another large camp, the Gila River Relocation Camp, was located 30 miles south of Phoenix on the Pima Indian Reservation.

THE BOOM YEARS

With the ongoing dam and irrigation projects and the wartime boom, Arizona flourished. But it was the invention of evaporative coolers that really allowed the state to blossom. These inexpensive metal boxes could cool Arizona's dry, hot air by sucking in the air, pushing it through a wet pad and then pushing it out again. Much cheaper than air conditioning, evaporative coolers made living in the state during its hottest months much more tolerable. Before evaporative coolers were mass-produced in the 1950s, Phoenix was primarily a winter retreat. These devices made the city livable year-round. In 1950, 107,000 people lived in Phoenix. By 1960 the city was bursting at the seams with four times as many people.

The Arizona sunshine beckoned to people in the cold, rainy north. Families, retired folks, and businesses moved south. As more houses were built, cities grew in the deserts, and canals were constructed to bring water hundreds of miles from the Colorado River to supply their needs.

At the end of the twentieth century, the state's population reached more than 5 million, as people continued to flock to Arizona, where it seems like the sun always shines.

THE NAVAJO CODE TALKERS

During World War II, the United States had a problem. The only way for troops to communicate during battle was to send coded messages by radio, but the Japanese were breaking the codes as fast as Americans could develop them.

Then someone got the idea of creating a code from Navajo, a language so difficult that at the time, only about thirty non-Navajo could speak it. Twenty-nine Navajo Marines came up with hundreds of code words for military terms and for letters of the English alphabet. They memorized them and practiced them until they could send and translate coded messages perfectly.

No one ever broke the Navajo code. "It sounded like gibberish," said one code expert. "We couldn't even transcribe it, much less crack it." Even other Navajo speakers couldn't make heads or tails of it.

In all, four hundred Navajo became code talkers. Military commanders used them to send orders and to warn Allied troops when they were in danger. The code talkers saved countless lives. In addition to the Navajo, there were also eleven Hopi code talkers.

The code talkers' finest moment came during the battle for the tiny South Pacific island of Iwo Jima. In the first two days of the invasion, six code talker units worked around the clock, sending eight hundred messages without a single mistake. The U.S. Marines finally took control of the island after a month of fierce fighting, marking a turning point in the war. "Were it not for the Navajos," says Major Howard Conner of the Fifth Marine Division, "the Marines would never have taken Iwo Jima."

NEW CENTURY ON THE BORDER

As the new millennium began, Arizona found itself facing a major challenge. After the terror attacks of September 11, 2001, securing the nation's borders became a priority, and Arizona, with more than 300 miles of land bordering Mexico, received increased scrutiny. The state had already begun working on curbing illegal immigration and drug smuggling, but Arizona's border was the site of most of the illegal activity along the United States–Mexico border. More than one-half of all apprehensions by the U.S. Border Patrol occur in Arizona. In addition to policing the border, state officials had to consider how to secure its large cities—Phoenix and Tucson—and to be better prepared for any type of disaster.

A U.S. Border Patrol agent in Sasabe, Arizona, transports illegal immigrants to a processing center.

One of the state's initial efforts was to create an antiterrorism task force and set up a special council to work with the U.S. Department of Homeland Security to eventually establish the Arizona Department of Homeland Security. In 2006 Arizona received a helping hand from the federal government with Operation Jump Start. National Guard troops were sent to four southwestern states—Arizona, California, New Mexico, and Texas—to support the U.S. Border Patrol.

The added troops led to a decrease in illegal border crossings, but not all of the security measures have been well received. As part of the Secure Fence Act of 2006, Congress and President George W. Bush approved the construction of a 700-mile fence covering several sections of the nation's border with Mexico, including much of the southern edge of Arizona. The Tohono O'odham Nation, located in the south-central part of the state, had already struggled with illegal immigrants, smugglers, and border patrol agents traveling on their lands for years. The Tohono O'odham were further dismayed by the fence, which they feared would negatively affect several of their cultural sites. The fence was also set to run through the Buenos Aires National Wildlife Refuge, in Sasabe, Arizona generating concern among some environmentalists.

Overall being located on the United States–Mexico border has put a strain on the state's resources and personnel. In 2007 Leesa Berens Morrison, the state's director of Homeland Security, called for increased federal funds for first responders to help create a safer, more secure Arizona. "Every day they address the repercussions of an open border," she told a subcommittee of the U.S. House of Representatives' Homeland Security Committee.

Today security remains a challenge for Arizona. Approximately 1,100 people per day are caught illegally crossing the national border in Arizona.

Chapter Three

The Good Life

So many people have poured into Arizona in recent years that Arizonans sometimes joke that anyone who has been there more than fifteen minutes is a native. But for every person who arrives in Arizona looking to start over, another is already there, trying to hold on to the cherished past.

NEW ARRIVALS DAILY

Arizona's population has been growing by leaps and bounds for decades. The state's population exploded between 1990 and 2000, from more than 3.6 million to slightly more than 5.1 million—a staggering 40 percent increase. Only one other state grew more quickly: Arizona's neighbor to the northwest, Nevada.

And Arizona's growth shows no signs of slowing. Its population grew another 23 percent between 2000 and 2006 to more than approximately 6 million residents. Many people come for the weather, others because they see beauty in the harsh landscape. Still others fall for the romance of the West, dreaming of freedom or a new start or a chance to live closer to the land.

With so much to offer, Arizona is receiving newcomers in great numbers.

Many of the people who have moved to Arizona in the last fifty years are elderly. Some are so-called snowbirds—northerners who head south to live when the snows come. They enjoy the sunny Arizona winters and then head north again in spring. When they descend on a quiet Arizona town, it's an amazing sight. In summer more than three thousand people live in the town of Quartzsite, near the California border. In winter Quartzsite's population tops 1.5 million. Not everyone stays the whole winter. "RVs suit our lifestyle," says one senior. "We're just active kind of people. After a few weeks we want to move on."

Others buy homes in towns built specifically for senior citizens. With more than 40,000 residents, Sun City, west of Phoenix, is one of

Many seniors escape the winter by living in Arizona's warm, dry climate.

the nation's largest retirement communities. Places like Sun City offer more than just houses. They have swimming pools, golf courses, arts centers, and weight rooms. "We're in the fitness center five days a week," says a retired dentist. "We're also learning how to oil paint and doing some pottery. There's enough options to choke a horse." "There's not much retiring going on here," chortles an elderly woman.

Most recently Arizona has experienced a wave of people moving from California, especially the southern part of the state. Many come for the more affordable housing prices and the lower cost of living. Kyle Campos moved from Santa Barbara to the Phoenix area in 2004. In California most homes in his area cost at least $1 million. In Arizona, he says "I could build my dream house for less than $300,000." Many members of his family have also relocated to the Phoenix area. With all its new residents, Maricopa County—where Phoenix is located—is the fastest-growing county in the United States. According to the U.S. Census Bureau, the county's population grew by 696,000 people between 2000 and 2006, to 3.8 million residents.

ETHNIC AND CULTURAL DIVERSITY

Although cultural diversity is increasing in Arizona, about 87 percent of Arizonans are white. Most have German, English, and Irish backgrounds. During the nineteenth century, many of their ancestors came to Arizona to work in the copper mines, as did some Italians and Serbs.

American Indians are the second-largest racial group in the state, making up 5 percent of the population. African Americans make up about 4 percent of the state's residents. In terms of cultural heritage, 29 percent of residents identify themselves as Hispanic, and more than 20 percent of these people say that they are of Mexican descent.

ETHNIC ARIZONA

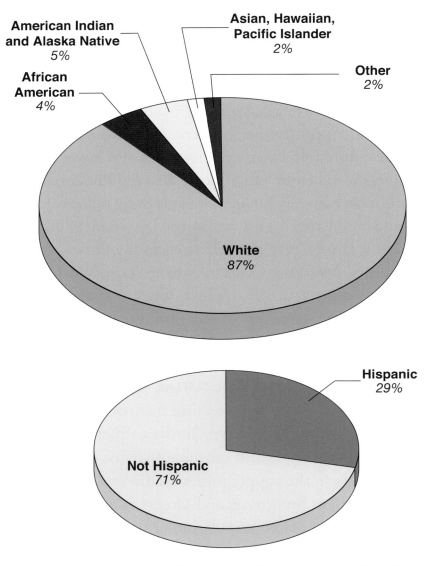

American Indian
and Alaska Native
5%

Asian, Hawaiian,
Pacific Islander
2%

African
American
4%

Other
2%

White
87%

Hispanic
29%

Not Hispanic
71%

*Note: A person of Cuban, Mexican, Puerto Rican, South or Central American,
or other Spanish culture or origin, regardless of race, is defined as Hispanic.*

The language and religions of Arizona mirror those of many other states across the country. English is the main language of the state, but Spanish is also prevalent. This is no surprise, considering that the state shares a border with Mexico. Spanish is spoken at home by almost 26 percent of Arizonans. More than one-half of the state's residents identify themselves as a member of some branch of Christianity, and most are Baptist and Catholic.

Once thought of as the Wild West, Arizona has grown up around its cities. More than 88 percent of the state's residents live in urban areas. With an estimated 1.5 million people in 2007, Phoenix is now the fifth-largest city in the country. To its south Tucson is also thriving. The once-dusty desert town had more than 518,000 inhabitants in 2005.

NATIVE ARIZONANS

Although many Arizonans are newcomers, many others are from American-Indian families who have lived there for centuries. Arizona has one of the highest American-Indian populations of any state. Six out of ten of the largest U.S. Indian reservations are located completely or partly within the state. The Navajo Nation alone has 104,656 residents. Its vast reservation, which spreads from northeastern Arizona into Utah and New Mexico, is larger than West Virginia.

This Navajo girl is one of more than 100,000 who live in Arizona.

Other native peoples in Arizona include the Apache, Hopi, Yavapai, Hualapai, Havasupai, and Tohono O'odham peoples. In all twenty-two separate tribes in Arizona are recognized by the federal government.

THE BIRTH OF BUTTERFLIES:
A TALE FROM THE TOHONO O'ODHAM

One day the Creator was relaxing, watching a group of children play. As the children cavorted and sang, the Creator grew sad. He realized that one day the children would grow old. Their hair would turn gray and their strength would fail, just as everything eventually withers and dies. Flowers shrivel and leaves fall from trees. The Creator grew even sadder at this thought, for winter was approaching. Soon the cold would set in, and no flowers or leaves would brighten the landscape.

But it was not yet winter. The sun was still shining. The sky was blue, yellow leaves were wafting gently to the ground, and women were grinding white corn into meal. Purple and red flowers spouted here and there. The Creator smiled. "I have to preserve these colors," he thought. "I will make something for the children to enjoy."

So the Creator took his bag and began filling it. He put in a handful of sunlight, some blue from the sky, a bit of white from the corn, some lines of black from a child's hair, yellow from leaves, green from pine needles, and purple from flowers.

After putting all the colors he could find into the bag, he gave it to the children, saying, "This is for you. Open it."

When they opened the bag, hundreds of colorful butterflies emerged, flitting and fluttering around the children's heads. Their eyes grew wide and smiles spread across their faces, and the Creator's heart lifted.

Many Arizona Indians have tried to maintain their tribal traditions. For instance, the Tohono O'odham, who live in the Sonoran Desert, were traditionally masters at gathering food in the seemingly inhospitable land. Over the course of each year, they collected the fruit and seeds of 375 different plants, some of which were only available for a few days. Although many Tohono O'odham still live in the desert, today they are much more likely to get their food from supermarkets. But many still use long sticks to pick the fruit that grows atop the saguaro cacti. They make this fruit into jelly, much as their ancestors did.

Likewise some Navajo still tend sheep, just as their parents and grandparents did. They pass on to their children the knowledge of how to weave the beautiful rugs for which the Navajo are famous. Of course, many other Navajo have left behind the traditional rural ways for opportunities in the cities. "Our jobs took us away from the sheep," states Betty Reid, a Navajo journalist who lives in Phoenix. "Asphalt, air pollution and the American Dream replaced the wide views, sage-scented air and nomadic ways."

Each September, the Navajo honor the old ways and the new at the Navajo Nation Fair, the world's largest American-Indian fair. For seven days, the town of Window Rock crackles with energy, as Indians and non-Indians enjoy rodeos, parades, and exhibits of jewelry, blankets, and other crafts. Some of the most popular

The annual Navajo Nation Fair in Window Rock, Arizona, includes traditional dances and other celebrations of American-Indian culture.

events are the traditional dance competitions. Visitors can also taste traditional Navajo foods, such as mutton and fry bread.

AFRICAN AMERICANS IN ARIZONA

The first person of African descent to arrive in Arizona is believed to be Esteban (sometimes spelled Estevan), a slave who acted as a guide for a Spanish expedition in the 1530s. Not until the 1800s did the state start to develop a substantial African-American population. Some blacks migrated to Arizona to work as cowboys, because the Wild West offered them more freedom than the Old South. Others migrated to Arizona to work in the state's many cotton fields. By the mid-1900s African-American communities were established in some of Arizona's cities.

African Americans in Arizona have fought hard for their civil rights. From the 1940s to 1960s they organized sit-ins and demonstrations that called for an end to racial segregation and discrimination. Although a 1954 U.S. Supreme Court ruling ended school segregation, discriminatory practices in public places, such as restaurants and movie theaters, continued into the 1960s.

In 1972 Clovis Campbell Sr. broke new ground as the first African American elected to the state senate. Yet there were still some hurdles to overcome. Campbell tried to get Arizona legislature to establish a holiday to honor Martin Luther King Jr., but the measure failed to pass several times. Not until 1992 did Arizona voters approve a holiday for the late civil rights leader. Today Martin Luther King Jr. Day is celebrated with special events, including children's activities and concerts. Another important African-American holiday is Juneteenth, which celebrates the end of slavery. Cities such as Tucson, Phoenix, and Yuma hold annual festivals with music, food, and activities to mark this important occasion.

The MLK Praise Dancers perform during Arizona's Martin Luther King Jr. Day cele-bration in Phoenix.

POPULATION DENSITY

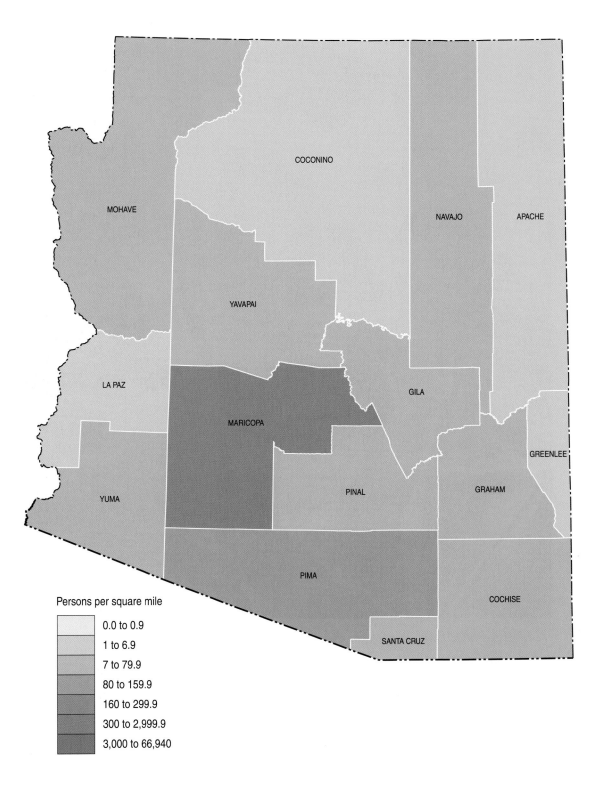

Persons per square mile

- 0.0 to 0.9
- 1 to 6.9
- 7 to 79.9
- 80 to 159.9
- 160 to 299.9
- 300 to 2,999.9
- 3,000 to 66,940

HISPANIC AMERICANS IN ARIZONA

Arizona is home to more than 1.6 million Hispanic Americans. Like American Indians, many of them have roots that go back to when Arizona was part of Spain. "It's so funny when people ask me when my family immigrated to the United States," says Gloria Medina, who comes from a family of ranchers near Tucson. "They don't understand that many of us have been here all along." Other Mexicans have arrived more recently, as have Puerto Ricans, Cubans, Nicaraguans, and Guatemalans.

Each May 5 many Arizonans celebrate *Cinco de Mayo,* which marks the victory of the Mexicans over the French at the Battle of Puebla in 1862. Cities and towns across the state hold special events to honor this important day. In addition to enjoying delicious Mexican food, attendees can watch

The Mexican women's horse drill team wait to perform at the La Corona rodeo in Phoenix.

GUACAMOLE

Mexican food is so popular in Arizona that Tucson once proclaimed itself the Mexican food capital of the world, apparently forgetting about the nation to the south.

Guacamole is a quick and delicious dish that can be eaten with chips or with any Mexican food. Have an adult help you with this recipe.

    2 soft, ripe avocados
    1 chile
    1 tomato
    2 tablespoons minced onion
    juice from 1/2 lime
    1/2 teaspoon salt

Peel the avocados and remove the pits. Mash the avocado with a fork, leaving some small chunks. (Guacamole should not be smooth.) Slice the chile in half lengthwise and throw away the seeds. Mince the chile and chop the tomato. Mix these and the onion with the avocado. Squeeze the lime juice into the mixture. Add salt.

Your guacamole tastes best when eaten right away, so grab some chips and enjoy.

men and women in traditional costumes perform folk dances as part of the day's festivities. Another holiday celebrated in Arizona and Mexico is Mexican Independence Day. On September 16 each year some communities remember the first day of Mexico's fight for independence from Spain with special celebrations. These colorful parties echo with mariachi music and fireworks.

ASIAN AMERICANS IN ARIZONA

Many Asian immigrants have also made their homes in Arizona. Chinese people began moving to Arizona during pioneer times to build the railroads. Some settled in towns such as Prescott and Phoenix, establishing laundries and other small businesses. In the twentieth century Japanese, Koreans, Vietnamese, and Laotians have also moved to Arizona.

In 1946 Phoenix lawyer Wing F. Ong, who had emigrated from China as a teenager, became the first Chinese American in the country to win elective office when he won a seat in the Arizona House of Representatives.

Asian-American Arizonans celebrate their rich heritage with events throughout the year. Phoenix honors Japanese culture with a festival called *Matsuri,* where you can see demonstrations of many Japanese traditions, from origami to martial arts. The Arizona Asian Festival is held in Phoenix and features arts and crafts, dance, and music representing numerous Asian and Pacific Island cultures.

THE ACTIVE LIFE

Newcomers and old-timers, seniors and teens—it seems that everyone in Arizona loves the great outdoors. Skiing, rock climbing, and bicycling all have their enthusiasts. Golf is another favorite outdoor activity. Each year,

11 million rounds of golf are played on more than 180 golf courses in the Phoenix area.

Although Phoenix gets just 7 inches of rain a year (the area is known as the Valley of the Sun), it abounds with pools, fountains, and artificial lakes. Some people question whether this is a wise way to live in a desert. They wonder how long the dams and canals

Boaters flock to Lake Havasu, enjoying the weather and water.

and pumps can keep the booming area supplied with water. But most people simply enjoy it. "If you're in the desert, you want an oasis," says one valley resident. Whether they are swimming, boating, or waterskiing, Arizonans take full advantage of the water. "I fish year-round, and I'm on the lakes year-round," boasts one. For many this lifestyle was what drew them to Arizona. As one Phoenix man says, it's "no-brain, no-hassle living."

THE COST OF GROWTH

With its ever-expanding population, Arizona's budget must be stretched further to provide necessary government resources to its people. More than one-quarter of its residents are younger than eighteen, so great demands are placed on the state's education system and child services. More than one million students are enrolled in Arizona's schools. With a tight budget, the state cannot fund all of its educational programs, and its teachers are underpaid compared with their peers in other states. For the 2004–2005 school year, for example, the average salary for an Arizona teacher was $39,095, well below the national average of $47,602.

By 2008 the average salary rose to $42,967, but it still trails salaries in most parts of the country. "We lose many, many great teachers who find they can make more money in other occupations and who can't afford to make the sacrifice," says Tom Horne, state superintendent of public instruction.

As its population grows Arizona must also contend with a significant amount of crime. In 2005 the Arizona Criminal Justice Commission released a report that indicated that the state had one of the highest crime rates in the nation, and the U.S. Census Bureau listed Arizona as having the sixteenth-highest rate of violent crimes that same year.

In addressing crime Arizona has looked to a number of high-tech solutions. To tackle car theft it has installed license plate readers in some police cars. These devices scan the letters and numbers on a car's license plate and then check to see whether the car is stolen or if its owner is sought by the police for any other reason. The state also began expanding a facility in Tucson to help with its criminal investigations. The Southern Regional Crime Laboratory processes evidence relating to a variety of crimes using several methods, including blood and DNA analysis.

In the coming decades Arizona will need to seek more innovative solutions to handle the growing needs of its people.

Chapter Four

Making Laws

Before it became a state, Arizona had to draft a constitution to establish the rules and principles by which it would be governed. When President William Taft saw the document, he was disturbed. The proposed constitution included a clause that allowed voters to recall judges—remove them from office. Taft, a former judge, refused to allow Arizona to be admitted to the Union until this clause was removed. But Arizonans expect to have a say in their government, and they don't like being pushed around. So in the very first election after Arizona became a state, the recall rule was voted back in.

INSIDE GOVERNMENT

Like the federal government the Arizona state government is divided into three branches: the executive, legislative, and judicial.

Executive

The head of the executive branch is the governor, who is elected to a four-year term. The governor is responsible for appointing important officials, proposing a state budget, and focusing attention on issues that he or she thinks are important.

Now open as a museum, this building once served as the Capitol of the Arizona Territory and later the State Capitol.

In 1998 Arizona voters made U.S. history when they elected women to the state's top five executive branch offices. In addition to Governor Jane Dee Hull, a woman was also elected secretary of state, attorney general, treasurer, and superintendent of public instruction. During the election Arizonans paid little attention to the gender of each candidate. Even after the four Republicans and one Democrat were elected, the occasion caused little fanfare. Gender did not seem to influence voters the next time around, either.

Jane Dee Hull won the state's top executive post in 1998.

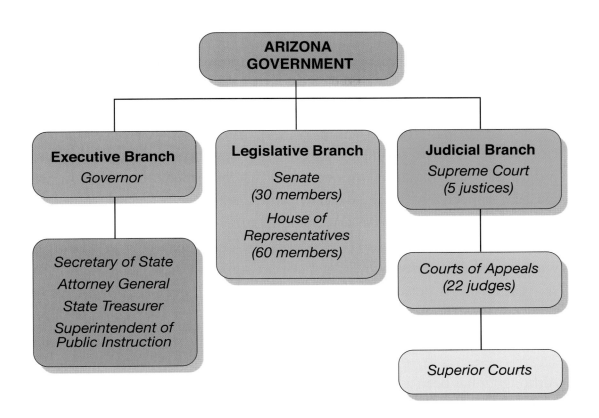

The one Democrat, Janet Napolitano, who had earlier been elected attorney general, succeeded Hull as governor in 2003.

Legislative

The Arizona legislature is composed of a thirty-member senate and a sixty-member house of representatives. Each senator and representative is elected for a two-year term. The legislators make new laws and change old ones. After a proposed law is approved by both houses, it is sent to the governor. The bill becomes law if the governor signs it, but he or she can also veto, or reject, the bill. Such a bill would then become law only if two-thirds of the members of both houses pass it again.

Judicial

The highest court in Arizona is the State Supreme Court. Its five justices are appointed by the governor to six-year terms. After that Arizona voters decide whether the justice should remain on the court.

In Arizona the most serious legal cases are usually heard in the superior courts of each county. The governor appoints the superior court judges in Maricopa and Pima counties, where Phoenix and Tucson are located, respectively. In the other counties, voters elect judges. A person who believes that a mistake was made in superior court can request that the case be reviewed by the court of appeals. This court has two divisions, with a total of twenty-two judges. All are appointed by the governor to six-year terms. A person who is dissatisfied with a court of appeals ruling can appeal to the State Supreme Court.

WILD WEST POLITICS

Although it has been a long time since the Earp boys strode the wooden sidewalks of Tombstone, public life in Arizona is still wild and woolly. People often have strong opinions. "The politics, it's just like the 1880s," says one woman from Tombstone. "At the city council meetings, people are always yelling and screaming at each other." Things got so rowdy that the city eventually passed a law fining anyone who makes trouble during these meetings. The only way to stay out of trouble, says this Tombstone resident, is to keep your opinions to yourself.

One Arizonan who was never afraid of telling anybody what he thought was Senator Barry Goldwater. In the 1960s most people believed that the government could make the country a better place. But not Goldwater. He believed in self-reliance. "I have little interest in streamlining government or making it more efficient, for I mean to reduce its size,"

Goldwater once wrote. "My aim is not to pass laws, but to repeal them." Although he lost the 1964 presidential election by a landslide, his influence has echoed through the years. He is considered the founder of the conservative political movement that has dominated American politics in recent decades.

Arizona senator Barry Goldwater speaks to a crowd in Boise, Idaho, during the 1964 presidential campaign.

Like Goldwater many Arizonans are individualists. They don't like anyone telling them what they can or cannot do. They don't like government regulations. And they don't like taxes.

As a result the state spends less money on education and programs to help the poor than most other states do. Arizona has one of the highest rates of uninsured children in the country, and it ranks close to last in the country in the amount it spends on each public school student. Governor Napolitano, however, hopes to improve those statistics. She has made children, education, and jobs her priorities since taking office.

IMPROVING EDUCATION

Although Arizona spends less per student than most other states, it works hard to provide quality education to its young people. To help its students start out on the right foot, Arizona has begun offering full-day kindergarten in some areas, and it eventually hopes to make the program available throughout the entire state. The extended school day for these young learners is intended to assist them with meeting growing academic demands and building essential skills for success in the years ahead.

The Arizona Department of Education wants to ensure that older students finish school. After years of double-digit high school dropout rates, the state began to turn the situation around in the early 2000s. A new position at the state's department of education focuses solely on dropout prevention, and the department has been providing grants to school districts and programs throughout the state.

Still the state needs to make more improvements to its educational system, according to a 2008 report from *Education Week*. It scored poorly in K–12 achievement and in its efforts to improve the quality of teaching.

Arizona's government places a high value on the education of the state's youth.

ARIZONA BY COUNTY

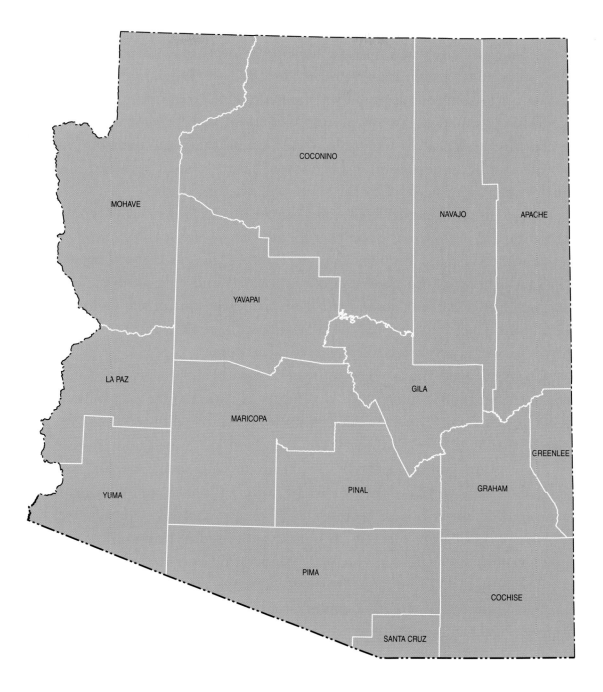

BATTLE FOR WATER

Another pressing concern for the state is the management of its natural resources, especially water. For decades this concern has led to conflicts with other states over Arizona's rivers. In 1922 the federal government stepped in to resolve a dispute over the Colorado River among Arizona, California, Nevada, Utah, Wyoming, Colorado, and New Mexico. The agreement, known as the Colorado River Compact, divided the river into two areas—the upper basin and the lower basin—and determined how much water could be used by the states in each area.

Although all the other area states signed the agreement, the Arizona legislature did not ratify the compact for another twenty-two years. In the meantime the federal Boulder Canyon Project Act of 1928 was passed. This act called for the construction of a canal and dam—which later became known as the Hoover Dam—on the lower part of the Colorado River. Some believed that this new construction project improved California's water access but adversely affected Arizona.

Conflict over the waters of the Colorado River resulted in a lengthy legal fight between Arizona and California. The case went to the U.S. Supreme Court, which, in its 1963 ruling, divided the lower part of the river's waters three ways. Out of the 7.5 million acre-feet, or 2.4 trillion gallons, of river water used each year, Arizona was granted 2.8 million acre-feet, or 912 billion gallons, while California received 4.4 million acre-feet, or 1.4 trillion gallons. Nevada was allotted 300,000 acre-feet, or 98 billion gallons. Anything above that total amount was to be shared equally between California and Arizona.

Despite this ruling concerns over the waters of the Colorado River have continued. In 2007 the involved states in the Colorado River Compact of 1922 met again to resolve their differences and form a

THE CENTRAL ARIZONA PROJECT

Around the same that time it ratified the Colorado River Compact, Arizona began exploring ways to develop and manage water resources in its central and southern regions. The result of this exploration was the Central Arizona Project, which called for a system of aqueducts and pumping plants and the creation of several dams. It was meant to serve farmlands in Maricopa, Pinal, and Pima counties; Indian lands; and the cities of Phoenix and Tucson.

But getting the necessary federal approval and funding for the Central Arizona Project took more than twenty years. The project was authorized in 1968 by President Lyndon B. Johnson, but construction did not begin until a few years later. The U.S. Bureau of Reclamation required environmental studies to assess the project's effects on the area's lands and wildlife. Finally, in 1973, the bureau started work on a canal from Lake Havasu to Tucson. When it was finished in 1993, it covered roughly 336 miles. A pumping station on the lake helps to start waters from the Colorado River on their journey southward. The cost of the project was more than $4 billion.

Today, more than thirty years after construction started, work still remains to be done. Several American-Indian communities have yet to be connected to the system and to receive their promised share of Colorado River waters.

MORE WATER TROUBLE UNDERGROUND

The Colorado River is not the only water source for Arizonans. Much of the state's water actually comes from underground pockets of water called aquifers. To meet the needs of farmers and residents, water is often mined from these areas. And as the population increases, so does the demand for water. Once all of the water is removed from an aquifer, the ground above it sometimes collapses. This drop in land elevation is called subsidence. Subsidence can also cause cracks or fissures in the ground.

Arizona has been wrestling with this problem for decades. In the late 1940s it was discovered that lands in south-central Arizona were sinking because of the removal of water from the aquifers below. By 1950 researchers noted that fissures had formed around the edges of the dropping water basins. One of the areas affected by subsidence was Luke Air Force Base, which had dropped 18 feet by 1992. Changes in land elevation can also cause flood problems. When the ground collapses suddenly, it can do a great deal of damage to roads, sewage and water pipes, and power and telephone lines.

State legislators have introduced laws to try to protect Arizona's water resources. In 1980 they passed the Arizona Groundwater Management Act, which sought to control the use of depleted aquifers, determine ways to share the groundwater fairly among competing groups, and develop alternative sources of water.

new agreement. The most recent pact provides a twenty-year plan for sharing the river's waters, and covers issues such as water conservation, water shortages, and droughts. It allows Arizona, Nevada, and California to save some of their allotments for later use in Lake Mead, the man-made lake created when the Hoover Dam was built. Aware that the Colorado River cannot provide enough water for its increasing needs, Arizona has pledged to find new ways to conserve water.

WE, THE PEOPLE OF ARIZONA

Although the legislature and the governor make many of the legal decisions regarding the state, the general public also has a say in Arizona's laws, programs, and other measures. Every election year voters are asked to select more than just their choice of candidates. They also vote on a number of propositions. To help voters understand the issues, the secretary of state's office assembles a huge packet of information covering all of the items that are up for vote.

In 2006 Arizona voters had nineteen propositions to consider. Some sought to amend the state's constitution regarding its official language, marriage laws, and taxes. Others called for a ban on smoking and the creation of an early childhood health-care program funded by a tax increase on tobacco products. The state's legislature also put two items directly in the hands of the people. Perhaps one of the most unusual propositions was Proposition 200, which sought to encourage people to vote by randomly awarding one voter in the state $1 million in the general or primary elections. Two-thirds of voters decided that the election lottery was not a good idea.

In addition to weighing in on propositions, Arizonans can create their own initiatives by collecting signatures and filing them with the secretary of state. They can also recall public officials through a petition drive.

Chapter Five
Making a Living

In the state's early days, its main sources of work were known as the five Cs: copper, cattle, cotton, citrus, and climate. Although many people are still employed in these fields, Arizonans work at many other types of businesses, too.

Arizona's first industry was mining, and it remains important today. Arizona produces more copper than all other U.S. states combined. Much of it is dug from the ground in giant open-pit mines. The Morenci Mine in southeastern Arizona is one of the largest open-pit copper mines in the world. It is an amazing sight: gigantic trucks at the bottom of the gaping chasm look like toy cars. Gold, silver, coal, sand, and gravel are also coaxed from the earth in Arizona.

Although few people think of Arizona as a farm state, it does produce many crops. It is one of the leading cotton-producing states and an important supplier of lettuce, melons, and citrus fruits. Arizona has approximately 10,000 farms occupying more than 26 million acres, according to a 2006 U.S. Department of Agriculture report. It is also home to many types of livestock, including cattle, pigs, and sheep.

Arizona's workforce is more than 2.6 million people strong in 2008. These steelworkers work on a copper refinery project.

Arizona farmers grow a variety of citrus fruit. This man harvests mineolas.

Another important part of the state's economy comes from its inviting climate and beautiful scenery. With its lakes and canyons, golf courses and ghost towns, Arizona has a booming tourist industry. Each year millions of visitors spend billions of dollars in the state. Although this results in many job opportunities at resorts, restaurants, car rental agencies, and the like, these are usually low-paying positions. Consequently many Arizonans are just getting by financially. "Tucson is generally a minimum-wage town," reports Charles Bowden, who writes about the Southwest.

Many people who arrive in Arizona discover that even for jobs that require additional training, wages are lower than they are in other parts of the country. For instance, after moving to Phoenix, a bookkeeper discovered that she would be making just seven dollars an hour instead of thirteen, as she did in Massachusetts. But for her, the Arizona lifestyle makes it worth it. "You get paid in sunshine," she says.

Arizona has started to catch up with the rest of the nation in salary levels, however. State workers made an average of $39,686 in 2006, about 5.5 percent below the national average but a marked improvement over the nearly 9 percent lower wages workers had to cope with a decade earlier. Some of the improvement can be attributed to companies hiring fewer workers but paying employees more. "You're going to have to pay for that talent," explains Don Wehby, senior economist for Arizona's Department of Economic Security.

Arizonans are also taking action themselves to improve their pay situation. In January 2007 voters chose to institute a state minimum wage for workers, which set the minimum hourly rate at $6.90 in 2008.

ARIZONA WORKFORCE

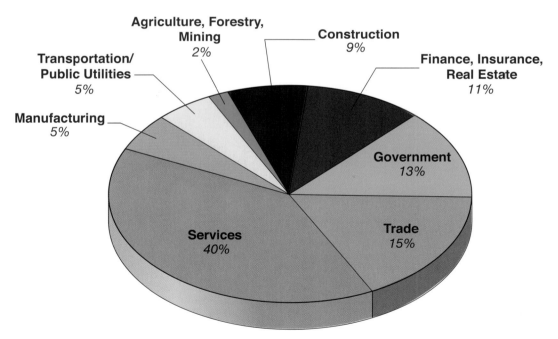

Agriculture, Forestry, Mining
2%

Construction
9%

Transportation/
Public Utilities
5%

Finance, Insurance,
Real Estate
11%

Manufacturing
5%

Government
13%

Services
40%

Trade
15%

THE LEGAL ARIZONA WORKERS ACT

In response to its struggle with illegal immigration, Arizona passed the Legal Arizona Workers Act in 2007. The act called for businesses to face penalties if they knowingly hired illegal workers. If the demand for such workers decreases, officials believe that the number of people entering the state illegally will also decline.

The law is considered one of the toughest of its kind in the country. The penalties are severe. A business can receive up to a ten-day suspension of its license and can be placed on probation for three to five years for a first offense. If the same business is caught knowingly hiring illegal workers a second time while on probation, it can lose its license permanently.

The law has many business leaders worried about its impact on the state's economy. One concern is that businesses might be deceived by illegal employees who might use false documents, causing the state to close the business for breaking the law. But the law requires businesses to use a special computer program created by the federal government, called E-Verify, to check out new employees.

Another worry is that the mere threat of punishment may drive businesses out of the state. This concern is shared by some state officials who admit that revoking licenses may be too harsh a penalty for such an offense. Others have objected to the act for legal reasons. They maintain that it violates an employer's civil rights because the employer has no way of responding to the state's charges. Despite several legal challenges, the law took effect in January 2008.

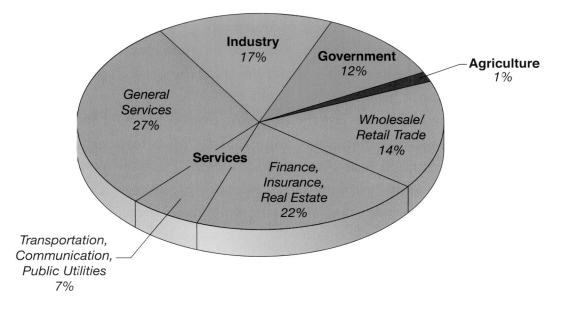

2006 GROSS STATE PRODUCT: $232 Million

- Industry 17%
- Government 12%
- Agriculture 1%
- General Services 27%
- Wholesale/Retail Trade 14%
- Services
- Finance, Insurance, Real Estate 22%
- Transportation, Communication, Public Utilities 7%

THE STATE OF BIG BUSINESS

With Arizona's ever-expanding population, it should be no surprise that many Arizonans work in the retail sales and service industries. In recent years one of the state's largest employers has been the national discount chain Wal-Mart. Bashas' Supermarkets and Home Depot are also among the state's leading employers.

Construction was a booming industry in Arizona for many years, but it started to slow down in 2006. The number of new homes being built decreased, but many people were still having trouble paying for the homes they'd already bought. Some took out large loans that they were unable to pay back. As a result the businesses that gave them the money for their homes, known as mortgage companies, began experiencing financial difficulties as well. Some went bankrupt, and this has created a nationwide problem.

Many lenders and banks in Arizona foreclosed on, or took back, the homes of residents who could not pay their mortgages. The number of houses in foreclosure in Maricopa County doubled from 2006 to 2007 from about one thousand homes a month to more than two thousand homes. Experts suggest that it will take years for the Arizona construction industry to bounce back.

Fortunately homes are not the only structures being built in Arizona. The state has a strong manufacturing industry. Most businesses in Arizona are concentrated near Phoenix and Tucson. Factories in the region churn out televisions, airplane parts, microchips, and even spacecraft. Raytheon Missile Systems makes military weapons in Tucson, and airplane manufacturer Boeing works on defense and research projects near Phoenix.

The computer industry also employs many Arizonans who develop software and design Web sites. The state offers special incentives to encourage the growth of such high-tech industries, including tax credits for small businesses.

This worker checks a yarn-spinning machine at a Yuma, Arizona, carpet factory.

EARNING A LIVING

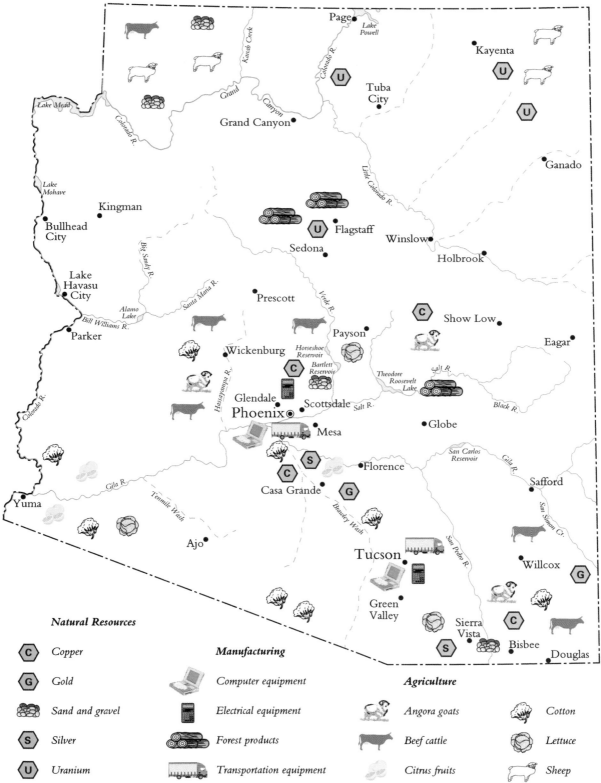

Natural Resources

C Copper

G Gold

Sand and gravel

S Silver

U Uranium

Manufacturing

Computer equipment

Electrical equipment

Forest products

Transportation equipment

Agriculture

Angora goats

Beef cattle

Citrus fruits

Cotton

Lettuce

Sheep

GOODS GOING ABROAD

Many goods from Arizona find their way to other countries. In 2006 the state exported more than $18 billion worth of goods. Equipment—electronics, machinery, aircraft, and spacecraft—is the biggest source of trade revenue. Cotton, vegetables, and dairy products are among the state's most sought-after agricultural items. Copper and related minerals are also one of Arizona's leading exports.

As a U.S. border state Arizona does most of its business with Mexico. The state formed a special organization known as the Arizona-Mexico Commission (AMC) to help build a strong bond between the United States and Mexico. The AMC works on improving trade relations and on issues related to its shared border.

After Mexico, Canada is Arizona's next-largest trading partner. Singapore, China, Malaysia, and the United Kingdom are also important buyers of Arizona goods. Governor Janet Napolitano has traveled to Canada and Great Britain to encourage more trade between her state and these countries. By developing good relations with other nations, Arizona is on its way to expanding its role in the world marketplace.

FUTURE CHALLENGES

In the line with the rest of the nation, Arizona faces some hurdles as the U.S. economy slows. The troubles in the housing market will have a lingering impact on the state. In an effort to ride out the economic turbulence safely, Arizona has been working on diversifying its economy.

In addition to encouraging new companies to move to Arizona and supporting small businesses, state officials have continued to build one of the state's most famous industries—tourism. They have hosted major events, such as Super Bowl XLII in 2008. Phoenix will host the NBA All-Star

Arizona tourism generates millions of dollars of income for the state. In 2006 visitors spent $18.6 billion.

THE GRAND CANYON: KEY TO PROSPERITY?

Although unemployment in the state has remained relatively low, this has not been true for Arizona's Indian reservations. The unemployment rate on some reservations, such as the Pascua Yaqui and the San Carlos Apache, has been higher than 20 percent in recent years. To boost their economies, these tribes and many others have begun operating casinos and other businesses.

On the other hand, the Havasupai have been looking to the land to improve their economic situation. They are trying to tap into the already strong market of tourists visiting the Grand Canyon's north and south rims. Their people have lived in and around the western edge of this great wonder for more than one thousand years.

Some Hualapai Indians are hoping to transform their unique location into an economic success story. The main feature of what they call Grand Canyon West is the Grand Canyon Skywalk, which allows visitors to see the canyon from 4,000 feet above its floor. A steel and glass U-shaped bridge with a glass bottom, the skywalk hangs over the lip of the canyon. Much of the funding for the project came from investor David Jin.

Construction of this unusual structure began in 2004 and was completed more than one year later. Designed to hold more than 70 million pounds and to withstand winds of more than 100 miles per hour, the skywalk opened in March 2007. Other attractions, such as a visitor center, museum, and restaurant, are in the works.

Game in 2009, and it hopes to bring more major sporting events to the state. Seeking to attract a special kind of visitor, the state formed the Arizona Governor's Commission on Film and Television to bring more actors and production crews to the state. With its breathtaking scenery, Arizona is a natural film star, having already appeared in hundreds of movies.

Encouraging innovation is another aspect of Arizona's plan for the future. Public and private organizations are joining forces to strengthen the state's economy. Science Foundation Arizona, formed in 2006, invests in a number of projects that unite businesses with researchers at educational institutions. These partnerships are meant to develop the state's science, engineering, and medical industries.

Chapter Six

Wild and Wonderful

Arizona is a big state with big attractions. No quick tour can include them all, but here are some highlights.

WILD WEST COUNTRY

"All you'll find will be your tombstone," someone warned prospector Ed Schieffelin when he headed to Apache country in 1877. Instead he found one of Arizona's richest veins of silver. Within four years, 10,000 people crowded into the brown hills near Schieffelin's claim, which he named Tombstone. The residents also took the name for the town that sprouted around the mines. By 1900, after the mines flooded, the population had dropped to fewer than one thousand and the price of silver dropped.

Today, with its wooden sidewalks and restored saloons, Tombstone holds tight to its history. Although visitors can watch reenactments of the gunfight at the O.K. Corral, the best way to get a sense of what life was like in the rough-and-tumble boomtown days is to visit the Boothill Graveyard. There you can read the matter-of-fact tombstones recording who was hanged and who was stabbed. With suitable dark

This group enjoys the Little Colorado River.

Tombstone, Arizona, is noted as being "The Town Too Tough to Die."

humor, one reads, "Here lies Lester Moore. Four slugs from a 44. No Les no more."

Not far from Tombstone is Bisbee, another mining boomtown. A huge supply of copper once lay beneath Bisbee's steep hills and gulches. So many people were busy digging copper out of the ground that by the early 1900s, Bisbee was one of the largest towns in Arizona. Today mining is history in Bisbee, but the town itself is pleasant and picturesque. Many buildings from Bisbee's heyday remain, clinging precariously to the hillsides.

Touring the Copper Queen Mine, where 8 billion pounds of copper were taken from the ground over the course of a century, is a fun way to learn about Bisbee's mining past. After receiving hard hats and yellow rain slickers, visitors climb aboard a mining car and head deep into the earth. The tours are led by real miners, who speak enthusiastically about their profession. "I love the smell of powder," says one after explaining methods of blasting. You'll learn lots of fascinating details on these tours, such as which animals were used to haul equipment underground. "They used mules," says the guide. "Don't talk to me about horses and ponies. They're too stupid. They don't duck if there's a low bridge. They bang their heads to pieces."

Southeastern Arizona also has a wealth of natural wonders. In Texas Canyon, huge boulders are piled atop one another, looking as if they will tumble down at any moment. For an even more amazing sight, head to Chiricahua National Monument, which contains whole forests of giant rock columns. On the park's many hiking trails, you can walk among the towering rocks, through huge archways, and past gigantic rocks improbably balanced on top of columns. You'll also pass some extraordinary plants, such as the alligator juniper, which has bark that cracks into little squares and resembles alligator skin as it spirals its way up the trunk.

The rock pinnacles at Chiricahua National Park are remnants of eroded layers of ash from a volcanic eruption 27 million years ago.

THE SONORAN DESERT

Lying along the Mexican border in the western part of the state, Organ Pipe Cactus National Monument is a long way from everything. But for beautiful, unspoiled Sonoran Desert, it's hard to beat. The monument takes its name from the organ pipe cactus, which grows only in this part of Arizona. You can see this desert giant, which has many large stalks shooting up from a single base, and a huge variety of other desert plants on hikes or bumpy drives through the rocky landscape.

The organ pipe cactus is rarely found in the United States, except on the lands of the Organ Pipe Cactus National Monument.

Although Tucson is a sprawling city, two of its best stops are dedicated to southern Arizona's extraordinary environment. You can bike, hike, or drive through beautiful stands of cacti at Saguaro National Park. Although a host of animals lives in the park, you're unlikely to see any creatures other than birds. Most of the resident animals venture out only at night, when the heat wanes. For a close-up view of some of these desert animals, head to the Arizona-Sonora Desert Museum, where you can say hello to tarantulas and scorpions, Gila monsters and mountain lions. You'll also get a good look at the amazing variety of cacti, wildflowers, and other plants that thrive in the Sonoran Desert.

Just south of Tucson is one of the most remarkable remnants of Spanish settlement in Arizona. San Xavier del Bac Mission is an ornate building, filled with scrolls and spires and statues. The current mission was completed in 1797. At the time no building within 1,000 miles was as elaborate or ambitious. Today it is still a strange sight in the Arizona desert.

Phoenix's one must-see site is the Heard Museum, the world's premier museum of the Southwestern Indians. You'll see intricately woven baskets, delicate pottery, and an amazing collection of Hopi kachina dolls. But the Heard is not just about the artifacts of American-Indian history. It is also about the lifeways and cultures of American Indians, past and present. You can walk into a cozy hogan, an eight-sided wooden building in which Navajo traditionally lived, or listen to tapes of Apache, Tohono O'odham, and others talking about their lives. You can even see artwork by contemporary American-Indian artists.

These kachina dolls are on display at the Heard Museum in Phoenix.

PLACES TO SEE

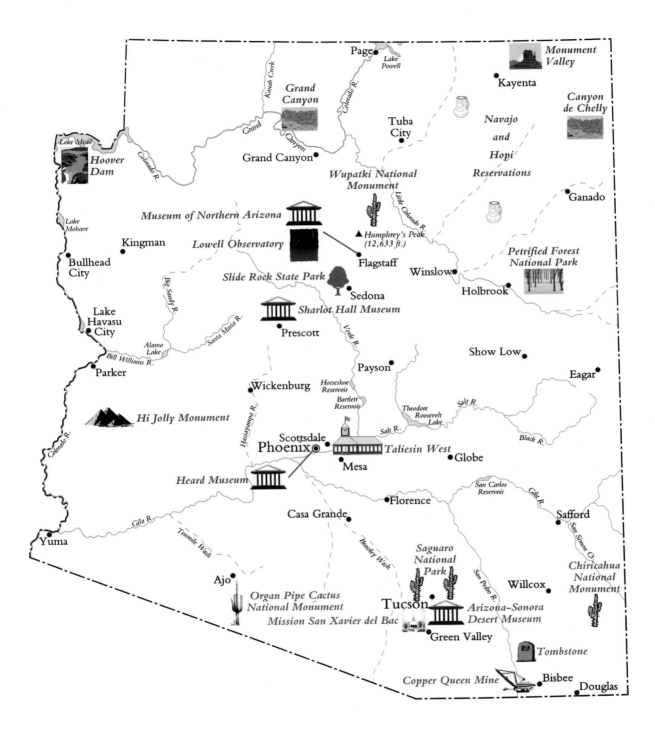

HEADING WEST

Driving westward out of the Valley of the Sun, visitors eventually come to Quartzsite, a rather nondescript town. The best reason to stop there is to see the Hi Jolly Monument. In the 1850s the U.S. Army tried to improve transportation across the desert Southwest. One experiment involved bringing eighty camels and several camel drivers from the Middle East. When the experiment failed, all the drivers but one returned home. Hadji Ali, whose name was pronounced "Hi Jolly" by the locals, stayed. After his death Hi Jolly was buried in a local cemetery under a huge pyramid topped by the figure of a camel—certainly one of Arizona's strangest sights.

Heading north, are the the brown, desolate hills of the Mojave Desert. Coming over the summit of a particularly steep hill is a massive structure. Hoover Dam is gigantic at 726 feet high and 660 feet across at its base, making it as tall as a seventy-story building and as thick as two football fields. The amount of concrete used to build it could have made a two-lane highway from New York City to San Francisco, California. Visitors learn lots of other facts about its construction on a tour of the dam.

The Hoover Dam generates 4 billion kilowatts of energy per year and provides flood control for the surrounding region.

LONDON BRIDGE

A logical person might assume that the London Bridge is in England. But Arizona is, after all, a place where lush lawns carpet the desert floor. Arizona isn't about logic; it's about dreams.

In 1964 Robert McCulloch was looking for a place to build a chainsaw factory. While flying across western Arizona, he spotted Lake Havasu. McCulloch decided that the lake was the ideal place for his new town. But how could he make Lake Havasu City different from all the other towns sprouting up in the Arizona desert?

When McCulloch heard that London was selling its famed bridge, he had his answer. The bridge, completed in 1831, could no longer handle the bustling city's traffic. McCullough bought it for more than $2.4 million and had it taken apart into 10,276 pieces and put back together again, halfway around the world in Arizona.

But having a bridge span nothing but sun-baked earth seemed rather silly, so McCullough had a channel dug beneath it. And what good is a beautiful English bridge that doesn't lead to anything? So up went shops designed in an old English style.

Now the London Bridge crosses an artificial river to a fake English village near a man-made lake. "It's fantastic what you Americans can do," an English visitor once said. "Where you don't have any history, you just make it."

TEN LARGEST CITIES

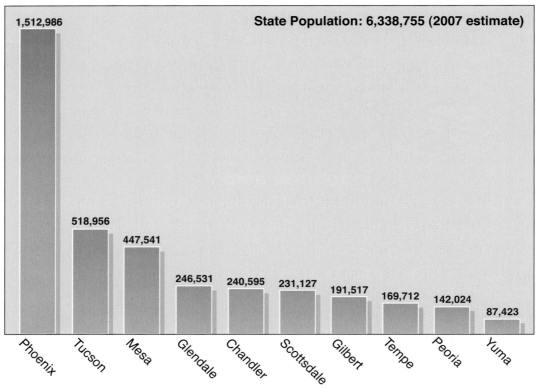

State Population: 6,338,755 (2007 estimate)

- Phoenix: 1,512,986
- Tucson: 518,956
- Mesa: 447,541
- Glendale: 246,531
- Chandler: 240,595
- Scottsdale: 231,127
- Gilbert: 191,517
- Tempe: 169,712
- Peoria: 142,024
- Yuma: 87,423

CENTRAL ARIZONA

Flagstaff, the largest city in northern Arizona, makes an excellent base for exploring the region's wealth of natural and historical wonders. But before heading out of town, stop by a couple of Flagstaff's sights that shouldn't be missed. At Lowell Observatory, learn what astronomers do, find out more about the galaxy with hands-on exhibits, and get a close-up view of the telescope that Clyde Tombaugh used when he discovered the dwarf planet Pluto in 1930. On some evenings the observatory allows visitors to look through one of its large telescopes.

Nearby the Museum of Northern Arizona is filled with fascinating exhibits about everything from how the Grand Canyon was created to how Ancestral Pueblo pottery changed over the centuries.

North of Flagstaff is Wupatki National Monument, where the ruins of several magnificent pueblos built by the Sinagua between 1040 and 1100 dot the desolate landscape. The largest of these, called the Wupatki Pueblo, was once three stories tall and contained one hundred rooms. Although the Sinagua abandoned Wupatki before 1250, some of their magnificent stonework is still intact.

Driving south from Flagstaff into the red rock country near Sedona will make your jaw drop. From the blinding red rock cliffs to the deep green pine forests to the glistening waters of Oak Creek, it is a magical place. With a dusting of bright white snow, the colors are phenomenal. Red rock country can be enjoyed in many ways. Just driving some of its spectacular roads will make visitors gasp at the glorious scenery. Hikers have their choice of a huge array of trails that head down refreshing creeks and past stunning formations such as Cathedral Rock or Devil's Bridge. In the summer, nothing can beat a trip down the natural rock slides into the swimming hole at Slide Rock State Park.

Farther south lies Prescott. Once the territorial capital, today it retains much of its early charm. The Sharlot Hall Museum was named for a poet who grew up nearby. When Hall was appointed territorial historian in 1909, she became

Slide Rock State Park, named for its slippery terrain, is a popular destination for many visitors.

the first woman to hold public office in Arizona. Hall's collection of historical artifacts and documents was eventually put on display in the Governor's Mansion, a log cabin built in 1864 as a home for the first territorial governor. Today the Sharlot Hall Museum is made up of several buildings. The Transportation Building is especially fun, with its old-fashioned high-wheeled bicycle and lavish stagecoach. And don't miss Fort Misery. Within a few years of its completion in 1863, this tiny two-room log structure served as the territory's first law office, first Protestant house of worship, first boardinghouse, and first courtroom.

Traveling south from Prescott, it is possible to trade the Old West for a glimpse into one man's vision of the future. Arcosanti, an experimental city and ongoing construction project, started in 1970 and is based on Italian architect Paolo Soleri's ideas about combining architecture and ecology. This "urban laboratory," as it's called, is located on a mesa at Cordes Junction. Among the massive concrete structures are apartments, businesses, and even a natural amphitheater—all designed to be environmentally friendly. Visitors tour the city, eat in its café or bakery, and take a look at the bells and other items made there.

INDIAN COUNTRY

Northeastern Arizona is Indian country. Most of the region is part of the huge Navajo and Hopi reservations.

On the edge of the Navajo Reservation is Petrified Forest National Park. At one time huge trees blanketed this region. Eventually these trees fell, and the logs became buried under dirt and volcanic ash. Water carrying minerals seeped into the logs. The water flowed on but the minerals stayed, attaching to the wood tissue. Over time the minerals built up until the trees turned to stone filled with colorful crystal patterns.

Visitors see many examples of petrified wood at the Petrified Forest National Park.

When tourism first sprang up in Arizona in the late 1800s, visitors carted away as much of this beautiful petrified wood as they could carry. "We had filled our hats with chips," wrote one visitor. "Oh such a time as we did have deciding which part of the forest to leave and which part to pack out." Indeed so many people packed pieces out—and carted off tons of huge logs on wagons or trains—that much of the forest was lost. Luckily the area was eventually placed under protection, and today visitors can walk among some of these mind-boggling petrified trees.

The barren pastel hills of the Painted Desert cover much of Petrified Forest National Park. The desert's reds, browns, purples, and blues come

The Painted Desert is a region that covers 93,533 acres. Various minerals and decayed plant and animal matter give the park its varied shades of color.

from the varying mineral content in each stripe of rock. The effect is particularly mesmerizing when the sun is low in the sky.

For hundreds of years, the Hopi Indians have made their homes atop three craggy mesas in what is now Arizona's northwestern corner. Walpi village has what is probably the most striking location of any settlement in Arizona. Sitting at the tip of one of these mesas, Walpi is more than 6,000 feet high. At one point the mesa narrows to just 15 feet across. Here you get the sensation of living in the sky, surrounded by nothing but the wind. Today few people live in the dusty village, which has neither electricity nor water, but it remains an important ceremonial site.

East of the Hopi mesas is Canyon de Chelly (pronounced d'SHAY), which many people consider Arizona's prettiest canyon. Its sheer cliffs often appear to be crumbling and delicate, and they are adorned with streaks that seem to drip down the reddish brown walls. To tour the canyon, visitors climb into the back of a big, blue open-bed truck for a wild, bouncing ride along the canyon bottom, right through the river that sometimes flows there. The trip takes you past soaring rock formations, ancient Ancestral Pueblo dwellings tucked into the cliffs, and even hogans where Navajo still live.

For sheer weirdness, few places can match Monument Valley. Its bright red buttes rise from the arid landscape like some otherworldly city. A scenic trip by car among the spires provides amazing vistas, but nothing can beat saddling up a horse and riding close to the monuments.

Driving west out of the Navajo Nation, be sure to stop at the Little Colorado River Canyon. From a distance it looks like a jagged scar running across the flat grasslands. Up close you can see that it is a slim canyon with sheer cliffs that drop to the trickle of water far below.

With its breathtaking scenery, Monument Valley is popular with filmmakers as well as visitors.

TO THE CANYON

Let's end our tour at the one spot where virtually every Arizona tourist visits. About 5 million people travel to the Grand Canyon every year. Most just spend a few hours here. They check out the viewpoints, peek over the edge, take some photographs, and watch the sunset.

But to really appreciate the canyon, you have to get into it. Hike down one of the trails and feel yourself dwarfed by the cliffs and pillars. Another option is to experience the Grand Canyon from the bottom. Some outfits offer mule rides down, and each year more than 24,000 people take boats along the Colorado River through the canyon. If you want to get away from the crowds, check out Edenlike Havasu Canyon, a side canyon to the Grand Canyon. Havasu Creek forms spectacular waterfalls as it rushes over red cliffs into blue-green pools far below.

No matter how you experience the Grand Canyon, it is worth the trip. It is, as President Theodore Roosevelt said when he visited the site in 1903, "the one great sight which every American should see."

Havasu Falls is located on the Havasupai Reservation within the Grand Canyon.

THE FLAG: *In the center of the Arizona flag is a copper-colored star, which represents the state's most important mineral. From the star radiate rays of yellow and red, the colors of Spain, which once controlled the region. The flag was adopted in 1917.*

THE SEAL: *Adopted in 1912, Arizona's state seal has images of mining, farming, and cattle ranching, which were once the state's most important economic activities. Above the scene is the state motto,* Ditat Deus, *which is Latin for "God Enriches."*

State Survey

Statehood: February 14, 1912

Origin of Name: Originally thought to have come from the Tohono O'odham Indian word *arizonac,* meaning "small spring," but many historians now believe that Arizona is taken from the Basque term *aritz onah,* which means "place of oaks."

Nickname: Grand Canyon State

Capital: Phoenix

Motto: God Enriches

Bird: Cactus wren

Flower: Saguaro cactus blossom

Tree: Paloverde

Mammal: Ringtail cat

Cactus wren

Saguaro cactus blossom

ARIZONA MARCH SONG

"Arizona March Song" was adopted by the legislature as the official state anthem on February 28, 1919.

Words by Margaret Rowe Clifford   **Music by Maurice Blumenthal**

Reptile: Ridge-nosed rattlesnake

Gemstone: Turquoise

Neckwear: Bola tie

Fossil: Petrified wood

Fish: Apache trout

Amphibian: Arizona treefrog

GEOGRAPHY

Highest Point: 12,633 feet above sea level, at Humphreys Peak

Lowest Point: 70 feet above sea level, along the Colorado River in Yuma County

Area: 113,634 square miles

Greatest Distance North to South: 389 miles

Greatest Distance East to West: 337 miles

Bordering States: California and Nevada to the west, Utah to the north, New Mexico to the east

Hottest Recorded Temperature: 128 °F in Lake Havasu City in 1994

Coldest Recorded Temperature: –40 ºF at Hawley Lake on January 7, 1971

Average Annual Precipitation: 10–13 inches

Major Rivers: Bill Williams, Colorado, Gila, Little Colorado, Salt, San Pedro

Major Lakes: Apache, Havasu, Mead, Powell, Theodore Roosevelt, San Carlos

Trees: Arizona oak, Colorado blue spruce, cottonwood, Douglas fir, juniper piñon pine, ponderosa pine, quaking aspen, white fir

Wild Plants: cholla, columbine, creosote, manzanita, ocotillo, phlox, prickly pear, saguaro, sand verbena yucca

Animals: badger, beaver, black bear, bobcat, Gila monster, javelina, mountain lion, mountain sheep, mule deer, porcupine, pronghorn, raccoon, rattlesnake, red fox, scorpion, tarantula

Birds: cactus wren, dove, eagle, Gila woodpecker, grouse, hawk, hummingbird, nuthatch, purple martin, quail, roadrunner, Stellar's jay, warbler, wild turkey

Fish: bass, bluegill, catfish, crappie, trout, walleye

Endangered Animals: black-footed ferret, bonytail chub, brown pelican, California condor, Chiricahua leopard frog, Colorado pikeminnow, desert pupfish, Gila chub, Gila topminnow, gray wolf,

Gray wolf

Hualapai Mexican vole, humpback chub, jaguar, Kanab ambersnail, lesser long-nosed bat, masked bobwhite, Mount Graham red squirrel, northern aplomado, ocelot, razorback sucker, Sonora tiger salamander, Sonoran pronghorn, Sonoran tiger salamander, Southwestern willow flycatcher, Virgin River chub, woundfin, Yaqui chub, Yuma clapper rail

Endangered Plants: Arizona cliff-rose, Arizona hedgehog cactus, Brandy pincushion cactus, Canelo Hills ladies'-tresses, Cochise pincushion cactus, Holmgren milk-vetch, Huachuca water-umbel, Kearney's blue-star, Nichol's Turk's head cactus, Peebles Navajo cactus, Pima pineapple cactus, Sentry milk-vetch, Zuni fleabane

TIMELINE

Arizona History

c. 1000 Hohokam, Ancestral Pueblo people (Anasazi), Mogollon, Sinagua, and other early Native American groups begin building complex pueblos in present-day Arizona.

1100–1400s The Navajo and Apache migrate into what is now Arizona; Hopi, Pima, Havasupai, Tohono O'odham, and other groups also live in the region.

1200–1450 The area's early American-Indian cultures disappear.

1539 Esteban (Estevan) becomes the first person of African descent to set foot in present-day Arizona when he crosses the region searching for the Seven Cities of Cíbola.

1540 Members of Francisco Vásquez de Coronado's expedition visit the Hopi while crossing Arizona.

1629 Franciscan priests establish a mission among the Hopi.

1687 Eusebio Kino begins missionary work among the Pima.

1752 Arizona's first European settlement is established at Tubac.

1776 Tucson is founded.

1821 Arizona becomes Mexican territory after Mexico gains its independence from Spain.

1848 Most of Arizona becomes a U.S. territory at the end of the Mexican War.

1854 With the ratification of the Gadsden Purchase, the United States takes possession of southern Arizona.

1858 Gold is discovered along the Gila River.

1859 The *Weekly Arizonan,* Arizona's first newspaper, begins publication in Tubac.

1862 Union and Confederate forces clash at the Battle of Picacho Pass in April.

1863 Arizona Territory is created.

1869 John Wesley Powell leads the first expedition down the entire length of the Grand Canyon.

1871 Arizona's first public school opens in Tucson.

1877 The Southern Pacific Railroad enters Arizona.

1881 The gunfight at the O.K. Corral takes place in Tombstone.

1886 Apache warrior Geronimo surrenders.

1912 Arizona becomes the forty-eighth state.

1922 Arizona refuses to sign the Colorado River Compact, an agreement on how to share the river's waters with other states; California, Nevada, Utah, Wyoming, Colorado, and New Mexico approve the agreement.

1936 American Indians in Arizona receive the right to vote.

1944 The Arizona legislature ratifies the Colorado River Compact of 1922.

1965 Lorna Lockwood becomes chief justice of the Arizona Supreme Court, the first woman to head a state supreme court.

1973 Work on the Central Arizona Project begins.

1975 Raul H. Castro becomes Arizona's first Mexican-American governor.

1981 Arizonan Sandra Day O'Connor becomes the first woman named to the U.S. Supreme Court.

1993 The canal from Lake Havasu to Tucson, part of the Central Arizona Project, is completed.

1998 Jane Dee Hull becomes the first woman elected governor of Arizona.

1998 Mexican gray wolves are reintroduced to the Apache-Sitgreaves National Forest in Arizona and the Gila National Forest in New Mexico.

2001 The Arizona Diamondbacks defeat the New York Yankees to win the World Series.

2006 National Guard troops are sent to Arizona to help the U.S. Border Patrol.

2008 Phoenix hosts Super Bowl XLII at the University of Phoenix Stadium; the New York Giants defeat the New England Patriots.

ECONOMY

Agricultural Products: barley, beef cattle, broccoli, cauliflower, cotton, dairy products, hay, lemons, lettuce, oranges, sheep, wheat

Sheep

Manufactured Products: aircraft parts, food products, newspapers, radios, scientific instruments, semiconductors, space vehicles

Natural Resources: copper, crushed stone, gold, sand and gravel, silver

Business and Trade: finance, real estate, tourism, wholesale and retail trade

CALENDAR OF CELEBRATIONS

Winterfest Skiing, snowmobiling, snowshoeing, sled dog races, sleigh rides, historic walking tours—there's something for everyone at this snowy festival in Flagstaff each February.

Matsuri: A Festival of Japan Each February, Japanese Americans in Phoenix honor their heritage with demonstrations of tea ceremonies, martial arts, sword dancing, and other activities. Visitors can also eat traditional Japanese foods such as sushi (raw fish) and yaki soba (fried noodles).

Gold Rush Days Travel back to the Wild West at this February celebration in Wickenburg. You can learn how to pan for gold, watch the bucking broncos at a rodeo, and check out a mineral show.

La Fiesta de los Vaqueros The world's largest nonmotorized parade—the floats are pulled by horses—kicks off this February rodeo in Tucson.

Heard Museum Guild Indian Fair & Market Each March, the Heard Museum in Phoenix hosts the Southwest's premier Indian cultural festival. On display is a huge variety of paintings, ceramics, and other arts. Visitors can also taste specialties such as acorn soup, an Apache dish.

La Frontera Tucson International Mariachi Conference For four days each April, Tucson is filled with the best mariachi music anywhere.

Rendezvous Days The lives of the mountain men—trappers and guides who lived in Arizona in the early nineteenth century—are remembered at this May celebration in Williams. Festivities include covered wagon rides, parades, dances, and a steak fry.

Prescott Frontier Days and Rodeo Each July Prescott proudly kicks up its heels at one of the world's oldest rodeos, which has been held annually since 1888. In addition to the rodeo action, visitors enjoy arts and crafts booths, a parade, and a spectacular fireworks display.

Navajo Nation Fair Each September, more than 200,000 people descend on Window Rock for the world's largest American Indian fair. Highlights include dancing competitions, livestock shows, rodeos, and jewelry displays.

Sedona Jazz on the Rocks World-class jazz performers travel to Sedona in September to play an outdoor concert in the spectacular red rock country.

Arizona State Fair This two-week extravaganza in Phoenix features everything from exhibits of rabbits to monster truck competitions. It takes place in late October and early November.

Arizona State Fair

Festival of Lights Boat Parade Dozens of decorated boats cruise Lake Powell each December, their lights dancing on the water.

STATE STARS

Edward Abbey (1927–1989), a novelist and essayist, wrote belligerent, funny books calling for the protection of the wilderness. Abbey first earned acclaim in 1968 for *Desert Solitaire,* about the year he spent working as a park ranger. His moving descriptions of the desert and arguments for its preservation inspired the environmental movement. In later books such as *The Monkey Wrench Gang* and *The Journey Home,* Abbey continued to urge people to fight for the wilderness. Abbey lived in Oracle.

Cesar Chavez (1927–1993) was a labor leader who led the first successful strike by California farm workers. Chavez, who was born in Yuma, was employed as a farm worker in his youth. In the 1950s he became a community organizer, putting together voter registration drives and helping people in their interactions with the government. Later his attention turned to labor organizing, and he founded what would become the United Farm Workers. In 1965 the union went on strike against California grape growers. Chavez organized an international boycott of California grapes in support of the strikers. After several years the grape growers finally signed contracts with the union. Never before had a farm workers' union in California obtained contracts.

Cochise (1812?–1874) was a Chiracahua Apache leader. In 1861 a false accusation that he had kidnapped a white child started a war. For several years Cochise led battles against U.S. troops, fighting to retain native land. He finally surrendered in 1871.

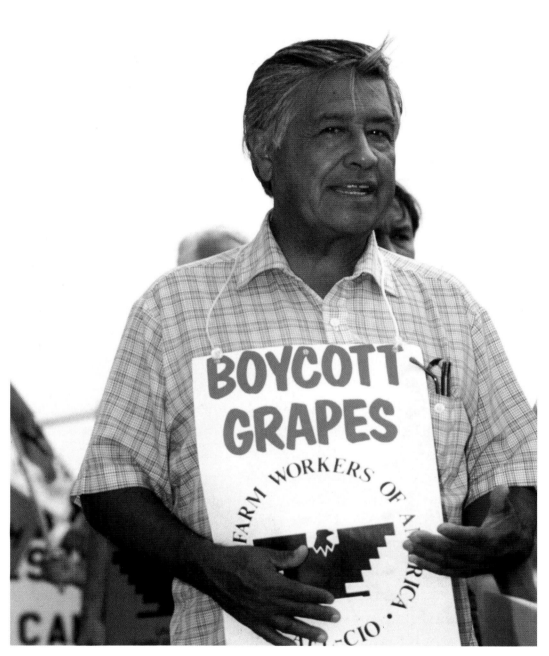

Cesar Chavez

Ted Danson (1947–   ) is an actor most famous for starring in the long-running television show *Cheers*. He earned two Emmy Awards for his portrayal of the baseball player turned bartender. The amiable actor has also appeared in films such as *Three Men and a Baby* and *Cousins*. Danson grew up in Flagstaff.

Geronimo (1829?–1909), a Chiracahua Apache leader, was born in what is now Clifton, Arizona. After his family was killed in 1858, he began raiding Mexican and American settlements. He became known as a great warrior. During the 1880s Geronimo led a band of renegades who refused to stay on the San Carlos Reservation. In 1886 he surrendered to white authorities and was sent to a prison camp in Florida. In his later years, he toured with a Wild West show.

Barry Goldwater (1909–1998) was a blunt-spoken politician who began the modern conservative political movement in America. Goldwater, a native of Phoenix, was president of his family's department store chain before being elected to the first of his six terms in the U.S. Senate. In 1964 he was the Republican candidate for president. Although he lost in a landslide, over time more and more people began to agree with his opposition to government spending and regulations.

R. C. Gorman (1932–2005) was born in Chinle on the Navajo Reservation. He was a leading Native American artist, famed for his free-flowing expressiveness. Gorman was one of the first American-Indian artists to incorporate European styles in his depiction of American-Indian subjects, which has made him very influential among younger Indian artists. He was also the first American-Indian to own his own gallery.

Ted Danson

Helen Hull Jacobs (1908–1997) was one of the greatest tennis players of the early twentieth century, famed for her speed and drive to win. She ranked among the top ten players in the world every year from 1928 to 1940, and won the U.S. National Championship four years in a row. Jacobs was born in Globe.

Eusebio Francisco Kino (1645–1711), a Catholic priest born in Italy, founded twenty-nine missions in northern Mexico and southern Arizona. Kino introduced cattle, sheep, and wheat to the region. He was also a mapmaker who gained fame for a map that showed that southern California was not an island, as Europeans believed.

Percival Lowell (1855–1916) was an astronomer who founded the Lowell Observatory in Flagstaff. Lowell, who came from a prominent Massachusetts family, spent his early career as a diplomat in Asia. In 1894 he set up a telescope in Flagstaff because it offered a clear view, far from city lights. He devoted the rest of his life to observing the planets. Lowell is most famous for claiming incorrectly that Mars held intelligent life and for predicting the existence of another planet in the solar system. This dwarf planet, Pluto, was discovered by astronomers at the Lowell Observatory after Lowell's death.

Charles Mingus (1922–1979) was an innovative jazz bassist and composer who changed how the double bass is played. Instead of using it just as a rhythm instrument, he played melody and percussion on it as well. In the 1940s and 1950s Mingus played with many jazz legends, including Louis Armstrong and Charlie Parker. He later led his own group, the Jazz Workshop. Some of his compositions, such as "Goodbye Pork Pie Hat" and "Wednesday Night Prayer Meeting," have become classics. Mingus was born in Nogales.

Charles Mingus

Sandra Day O'Connor (1930–) was the first female justice on the U.S. Supreme Court. O'Connor was born in El Paso, Texas, but spent much of her childhood on her family's ranch near Duncan, Arizona. She worked as a lawyer and assistant attorney general in Phoenix before becoming an Arizona state senator. Later, as a judge on the Maricopa County Superior Court and the Arizona Court of Appeals, she earned a reputation for fairness and hard work. In 1981 President Ronald Reagan made history when he appointed her to the Supreme Court.

John Wesley Powell (1834–1902) led the first expedition down the Colorado River all the way through the Grand Canyon. Powell, who was born in New York, lost an arm while fighting for the Union during the Civil War. Powell led expeditions through the canyon in 1869 and 1871–1872. His mesmerizing book, *Explorations of the Colorado River of the West and Its Tributaries,* made the canyon famous. Later Powell became head of the U.S. Geological Survey.

William Rehnquist (1924–2005) was chief justice of the U.S. Supreme Court from 1986 to 2005. Rehnquist, a Wisconsin native, set up his legal practice in Phoenix in 1953. He eventually began working for the U.S. Justice Department, and in 1971 was appointed to the Supreme Court. Rehnquist soon proved himself one of the court's most conservative members. In 1986 he was named chief justice.

Marty Robbins (1925–1982), one of the most successful country singers of all time, was born in Glendale. Robbins began performing in clubs around Glendale in the late 1940s, and by 1950, he had his

Sandra Day O'Connor

own television show in Phoenix. Robbins had hit after hit through the 1950s and 1960s. In 1959 "El Paso" reached number one on both the country and the pop charts. Robbins had ninety-four songs make the country charts, the eighth-highest total ever.

Linda Ronstadt (1946–   ) is a popular singer whose work has ranged from country to rock to opera to Latin. Ronstadt first hit it big with her 1974 album *Heart Like a Wheel,* which sold more than 2 million copies and produced a string of hits, including "You're No Good" and "When Will I Be Loved," that climbed both the pop and country charts. In 1987 Ronstadt recorded a Spanish-language album, *Canciones de Mi Padre* (*Songs of My Father*), which earned her a Grammy Award. Ronstadt, a native of Tucson, has won a total of ten Grammies.

Leslie Marmon Silko (1948–   ) is a critically acclaimed novelist and poet who explores the world of Native Americans. In her first novel, *Ceremony,* Silko weaves traditional Native American stories into her tale of a man trying to keep his sanity after returning home from the horrors of World War II. Another novel, *Almanac of the Dead,* deals with the long history of mistreatment of Native Americans. Silko lives in Tucson.

Louis Tewanima (c. 1879–1969) was a runner who held the American record in the 10,000-meter race for fifty-two years. Tewanima was born in Second Mesa on the Hopi reservation. He attended the Carlisle Indian School in Pennsylvania, where his graceful running was soon noticed. Tewanima won the silver medal in the 10,000-meter race at

Linda Ronstadt

the 1912 Olympics. In 1954 he was named to America's All-Time Track and Field Team, and three years later he was the first person inducted into the Arizona Sports Hall of Fame.

Morris Udall (1922–1998) was a highly respected politician who represented Arizona in Congress for thirty years. Udall was known for his sense of humor and his willingness to work with members of both parties. His accomplishments include helping to establish wilderness areas and working for campaign finance reform and civil rights legislation. Udall was born in St. Johns.

TOUR THE STATE

Monument Valley Navajo Tribal Park (Kayenta) A 17-mile scenic drive takes visitors past striking red buttes and spires.

Hubbell Trading Post National Historic Site (Ganado) Since 1878 Navajo have been bringing items such as rugs and jewelry to this post to exchange for food, tools, and other supplies. Besides seeing outstanding crafts, you can often watch artists at work.

Meteor Crater (Winslow) Nearly 50,000 years ago, a meteor slammed into Earth, creating this huge hole measuring 550 feet deep and more than 4,000 feet across. It is the best-preserved meteor crater on the planet.

Navajo Bridge (Lees Ferry) Brave visitors can walk across this narrow, 909-foot-long bridge that looms 470 feet above the Colorado River at Marble Canyon.

Meteor Crater

Pipe Spring National Monument (Fredonia) Get a taste of frontier life at this restored fort and ranch dating from 1870.

Grand Canyon National Park (Tusayan) This massive chasm, the most famous natural site in the United States, features stunning views and steep trails.

Sunset Crater Volcano National Monument (Flagstaff) The Lava Flow Trail at the base of this volcanic cone that last erupted about 750 years ago takes visitors past hardened, gnarled lava. Amazingly some plants have managed to grow in this strange moonscape.

Museum of Northern Arizona (Flagstaff) Exquisite Ancestral Pueblo pottery, colorful Hopi Kachina dolls, and a detailed display on the geology of the Grand Canyon are just a few of the draws at this excellent museum.

Jerome State Historic Park (Jerome) Located in a mansion built for James "Rawhide Jimmy" Douglas, the local mining king, this park will tell you all about the history of Jerome, an unusual town that clings to the side of a mountain.

Chapel of the Holy Cross (Sedona) This powerful modern church is built among the red rocks of Sedona.

London Bridge (Lake Havasu City) This bridge spanned the river Thames in London for about 140 years before being taken apart and transported to the Mohave Desert.

Heard Museum (Phoenix) You can check out a Navajo hogan, listen to Native American music, and even do your own beadwork at the leading museum of Southwestern Native Americans.

Desert Botanical Garden (Phoenix) People have been living in the Sonoran Desert for thousands of years. Find out how they used the unusual desert plants by making your own paintbrush out of a yucca frond or pounding mesquite beans into flour. You'll also find out how these plants have adapted to their severe environment.

Hall of Flame Museum of Firefighting (Phoenix) At this museum, you can climb aboard a fire engine from 1951 and get a good look at more than one hundred others. The Hall of Flame also boasts the world's largest collection of firefighting gear.

Casa Grande Ruins National Monument (Coolidge) The Hohokam built this massive four-story structure around 1350 CE. It is the largest prehistoric building in Arizona.

Yuma Territorial Prison State Historic Park (Yuma) After this prison was built in 1876 it became known as the Hellhole of Arizona. Touring it today, you'll hear stories of the men and women who suffered in its 120-degree heat and of their escape attempts.

Tonto National Monument (Roosevelt) Climb through the beautiful Superstition Mountains to see the ruins of buildings the Salado people built in a cave nearly seven hundred years ago.

Saguaro National Monument (Tucson) A drive through this park will take you past vast stands of towering saguaro cacti. In the early morning or evening, you might catch a glimpse of some of the many animals that live in the desert, such as roadrunners, jackrabbits, and desert tortoises.

Tombstone Pretend you're one of the Earp boys as you walk down Tombstone's wooden sidewalks, past buildings where bullet holes are still visible. The offices of the *Tombstone Epitaph,* the newspaper that chronicled all the mayhem, display the paper's original printing press and other memorabilia.

Tumacácori National Historical Park (Tubac) The ruins of this simple, weighty mission church built around 1800 evoke a time when Spanish missionaries were the only non-Indians in Arizona.

FUN FACTS

Sometimes it's hard to know what time it is in Arizona. It is the only state in the Union that doesn't participate in Daylight Saving Time. Each April (now March, as of 2007), Utah to the north and New Mexico to the east jump an hour ahead, but Arizona doesn't. The sprawling Navajo Reservation, however, does use Daylight Saving Time. To complicate matters further, the Hopi Reservation, which is completely surrounded by the Navajo lands, stays with the rest of Arizona on standard time. So when you go from New Mexico to Arizona in the summer, you lose an hour, but when you enter Navajo country you jump ahead an hour—and then you go back an hour when you cross into Hopi land!

Arizona is the site of the nation's largest mass escape from a prisoner-of-war camp. During World War II, German prisoners were held in what is now Phoenix's Papago Park. On Christmas Eve, 1944, twenty-five Germans escaped after having spent months digging a 180-foot-long tunnel. Three of them had studied maps of Arizona and had built kayaks, which they planned to sail down the Salt River to Mexico. Unfortunately for them, when they got to the river, it was bone dry. All of the escapees were eventually recaptured.

Find Out More

You can learn a lot more about Arizona at your local library. Here are some titles to get you started.

BOOKS

Bockenhauer, Mark H. and Stephen F. Cunha. *Our Fifty States.* Washington, DC: National Geographic, 2004.

Bruchac, Joseph. *Code Talker: A Novel About the Navajo Marines of World War II.* New York: Dial Books, 2005.

Iverson, Peter. *The Navajo.* Philadelphia: Chelsea House Publishers, 2005.

Lowe, Sam. *Arizona Curiosities: Quirky Characters, Roadside Oddities & Other Offbeat Stuff.* Guilford, CT: Globe Pequot, 2007.

McIntosh, Kenneth. *Navajo.* Broomall, PA: Mason Crest Publishers, 2004.

Seidman, David. *Cesar Chavez.* Danbury, CT: Franklin Watts, 2004.

Souza, D. M. *John Wesley Powell.* Danbury, CT: Franklin Watts, 2004.

Treat, Wesley. *Weird Arizona.* New York: Sterling Publishing Co., 2007.

WEB SITES

About Arizona for Kids

www.azlibrary.gov/links/kidsAZ.cfm

Created by the Arizona State Library, Archives and Public Records, this Web page provides tons of links to interesting information about the state.

Arizona @ Your Service

az.gov/webapp/portal/

The official Web site of the state of Arizona is chock-full of information about the state. It also has many useful links to other sites.

Arizona Kid Zone

www.arizonaguide.com/kidzone/Default.aspx

The Arizona Department of Tourism's site for kids offers games along with fun facts about the state.

Index

Page numbers in **boldface** are illustrations and charts.

ABOUT THE AUTHORS

Melissa McDaniel is the author of many books for young people, including *South Dakota* and *New Mexico* in the Celebrate the States series. To write *Arizona,* she traveled to every corner of the state, marveling at its fantastic landscape and fascinating history.

Wendy Mead is a freelance writer and editor. In her work, she has tackled a variety of subjects for young readers, from Arizona to alternative music, from birds to biographies. Mead has visited Arizona several times, and she enjoyed the state's hiking trails in Grand Canyon National Park and took a ride on the Colorado River from Lee's Ferry. She lives in Connecticut with her family.